C 8 E / 25

Wells Cathedral Revisited

A guided walk around the cathedral's tombs and monuments

A collection of tales and quotations relating to Bishops of Bath and Wells, and Deans of Wells Cathedral, from the Eleventh to the Nineteenth century, resulting in a tourist guide to their Graves, Tombs or Monuments in the Cathedral, to which is added a chronological table of their monarchs.

Compiled by Bill Welland

White Pheasant Publishing

ISBN 978-0-9933845-0-9

First published September 2015

Published by White Pheasant Publishing

Printed by The Somerton Printery Ltd.   TA11 6SB

Preface

If this is your first visit to Wells Cathedral, go on one of the excellent tours led by the cathedral's volunteer guides; or you will miss much of interest.

If you have already been shown around the cathedral, have watched the clock strike, and have admired the scissor arches, the Jesse window and the various remarkable column capitals, and are now wondering what stories the mitred effigies and other monuments could tell, then this is the guide for you. Here you will find some historical and biographical context for these tombs and monuments to bishops and deans who have been associated with this cathedral over the last 1000 years and more.

The first "guide book" to Wells Cathedral was *A Concise History of the Cathedral Church of St Andrew, in Wells* written by John Davis, one of the vergers, in 1809. That book, together with the 800-page *Lives of the Bishops of Bath and Wells from the Earliest to the Present Period* by the Rev. Stephen Cassan in 1829, provided the inspiration for this booklet, but we have used many other sources, as the bibliography will show.

As there are frequent disagreements between authors, what you read here may not always be true, but we will tell you who said it. Note also that the spelling of some names has changed over the years, so not all of the inconsistencies can be attributed to editorial flaws. Even the 'mural tablet' to Bishop Creyghton / Crighton uses two spellings of his name.

The plan of the cathedral on the inside of the covers is a modified version of Cattermole's drawing from the illustrated 1824 edition of Britton. Perhaps, one day, this booklet too will have a suitably illustrated edition.

The Appendix provides similar historical and biographical details for many more bishops and deans. In general the bishops it covers moved on (however briefly) to greater things after their time at Wells, and left the building with no monument to them.

Hardly anyone appointed after 1890 gets much of a mention in this booklet. There just aren't enough interesting stories about them in print.

To reach the starting point for this tour, enter from the west cloister and walk across the end of the nave.

Dean John Forest (1425-1446)

As you pass the main door you may be walking close to the grave of Dean John Forest, for in his will he asked for "the burial of my body before the great door … inside the church".

It may be that he didn't leave enough money to the cathedral for his successor (Nicholas Carent) to comply, though Hardy assures us that he "was buried in the cathedral".

His tomb was once thought to be elsewhere "inside the church", but is now lost. The most intriguing bequest in his will is to "the venerable Father, my most special prince and lord Henry Beauford, Cardinal of England and Bishop of Winchester, to buy one jewel for himself, 40*li*". Perhaps if he'd left that money to the church of Wells you'd now be looking at his grave.

Now walk up the north aisle of the nave until you pass the third pillar from the west end, then look across the nave.

At the tops of the two pillars opposite, you will see two busts. One is of a king holding a child upside down, and the other of a bishop with a group of people commonly supposed to be his family.

Although this booklet is mainly about bishops and deans, you will discover that their monarchs have often played a significant part in making them worth remembering, so the Appendix contains a large table showing which deans, bishops and monarchs were contemporaries.

These particular busts are from the 14th century, when married bishops were unknown, and Harington reports that "the old men of Wells had a tradition, that when there should be such a king, and such a bishop, then the church should be in daunger of ruine."

This tradition was not put to the test until the middle of the 16th century, when popular belief identified the king as Henry VIII, the child as the future Edward VI, and the bishop as William Barlow.

| Bishop |
| William |
| Barlow |
| (1548- |
| 1553) |

Barlow was appointed in 1548, just after Edward VI (the nine-year-old son of Henry VIII) had come to the throne, and in Harington's words was "the first maryed bishop of Wells, and perhaps of England." He was bishop here for only five years, during which there was indeed danger of ruin.

Edward's uncle was made Lord Protector, and Duke of Somerset. Collinson says the Protector became a great favourite with his young nephew, and after Somerset's army defeated the Scots in 1547, the king "extended his generosity towards him beyond the bounds of equity ... out of the lands and possessions of this bishoprick he bestowed on him a large gratuity."

Barlow (and the Dean and Chapter) permitted this, in exchange for the Duke's promise of £2,000 in compensation, but Collinson says this was a mistake, as "The Court, perceiving the Bishop so easy to be wrought on, and so complacent in giving up the revenues of his church, tried him still farther."

Certainly the result fits Harington's tradition, as "great havock was made with the buildings and revenues of the church. What with selling, exchanging, and spoiling, the see lost in a very few years nearly half of its possessions." Davis, similarly, saw Barlow as "a man of the most corrupt principles, having suffered nearly one half of the revenues of this church to be sold and exchanged, together with many buildings belonging to this See."

Britton contends that "the law, as it regarded the power of the Sovereign or his council, to make alienations, was equally as strong in Edward the Sixth's time as in Queen Elizabeth's; and Barlow could no more have resisted the will of Protector Somerset than many other prelates could that of the Queen." Fuller has a similar view: "others make his consent to signify nothing, seeing empowered sacrilege is not so mannerly as to ask any 'By your leave'."

Barlow fled to Germany in 1554, when the Protestant Edward died young and was succeeded by his Catholic half-sister Queen Mary. Although he did return to England when Mary died in 1558, it was to become Bishop of Chichester.

Barlow might be considered a serial bishop, as he appears to have held both St Asaph and St Davids before coming to Wells. Wood attributes the promotion from St Davids to Barlow's having become "a zealous professor and preacher of the reformed religion" despite his having been a Prior and an Abbot before the reformation. He also provides a surprising light on the other consequences of Barlow's marriage: "he had issue five daughters that were all married to bishops." These were two bishops of Winchester, and bishops of Hereford, Litchfield & Coventry and an archbishop of York. Wood doesn't mention the other coincidence - that both bishops of Winchester died within a year of their appointments!

Now walk a further four columns up the north nave aisle until you come to the little stone chapel fitted in between the next two columns. This is the chantry chapel built for Nicholas Bubwith.

Bishop Nicholas Bubwith (1407-1424)

Bubwith had briefly been Treasurer of England, Bishop of London and Bishop of Salisbury, but seems to have come good at Bath and Wells. He was responsible not only for his chantry chapel, but also for alms-houses, the Library, and even the north-west tower of the cathedral.

Henry V came to the throne in 1413, and he sent Bubwith as his principal envoy to the Council of Constance where, according to Britton, "he was one of the thirty ecclesiastics who were associated with the cardinals in the election of Pope Martin the Fifth." This election, in 1417, ended the Papal Schism which had previously resulted in three claimants to the papacy.

Bubwith's will asks for his body "to be buried in the church of S. Andrew of Wells in the tomb under the chapel which I caused to be made there for the chantries of certain chaplains to celebrate divine offices therein for my soul and the souls of my parents and benefactors by the grace of God for ever, according to the ordinance of me or my executors."

He also left a lot of money - "1000 marks to be expended upon the mending and repair of bad and deep ways within the county of Somerset", with another thousand for the building of "a new library over the Eastern side of the cloister" and "the construction or completion of the campanile or North tower at the West end … in all respects similar to the Southern tower there called 'Harewelstoure', on condition that the chapter duly pay the 300 marks which it granted to me for the said work … the said North tower forthwith be begun and on its completion be called and designated 'Bubbewithstoure'." [1½ marks = £1]

Not content with appointing several canons as his executors, he also appoints a supervisor: "the Reverend Father in Christ, and my most renowned Lord Henry by the grace of God Bishop of Winchester, Chancellor of England". Hidden under that long title is Henry Beaufort the former Dean of Wells and the future Cardinal Beaufort, notorious interrogator of Joan of Arc.

Looking into the chapel from the nave aisle you can see, in the far right corner, what Colchester calls "a square mousehole". Now read on.

A raised stage covers the nave beside Bubwith's chantry, but a few steps into the nave you can just see the corner of a floor-slab sticking out from under the stage. This probably marks the grave of Walter Haselshaw.

Bishop Walter Haselshaw (1302-1308)	Dearmer tells us that Haselshaw was "successively canon, dean, and bishop", and he is believed to have been dean 1295-1302, but Wharton's notes are unusually detailed in his case, and include the sentence: "Manet igitur difficultas inextricabilis de Petro de Insula."

Fortunately Hardy has translated and explains: "There is some inexplicable difficulty here. Documents are extant which state that Walter de Haselshawe was dean of Wells in June 1302; and yet Peter de Insula is also called dean of Wells. Wharton suggests that he is so called in mistake for subdean."

Certainly Malden makes no mention of Peter de Insula when he refers to "another period of great building activity: this time under three successive deans, Walter Hasleshaw, Henry Husee and John Godelee" Hardy's list of Archdeacons of Wells includes both Haselshaw and Peter de Insula, saying that Peter "had letters of protection" in 1295 and 1299 after Archdeacon Haselshaw had been advanced to Dean.

Britton says Haselshaw's slab "has been richly inlaid with brasses, but all are gone; the episcopal figure, in brass, was 10 feet in length", and Reid says an investigation in 1925 lifted the step of Bubwith's chapel and revealed part of Haselshaw's inscription. Colchester adds that cutting the square mouse-hole did reveal a letter 'E' of the inlaid inscription, but that this has since been lost. When you remember that the mouse-hole is visible above the floor inside the chantry, and the investigation lifted stones off the floor of the cathedral, it appears that Colchester has expressed himself badly, so let's turn to the primary source.

Connor explains: "It seemed unlikely that Haselshaw's brass would have entirely disappeared at the time of the building of Bubwith's chantry little more than a hundred years after it was laid down. To satisfy my curiosity the Dean was kind enough to give permission for the step (38 in. × 28 in.) into the chantry on the south side to be lifted. This was done on April 21st, 1925, with no very interesting results. No brass letters remained *in situ*, but the matrix of the word "QVONDAM" was sharply defined. On April 30th, with Sir Charles Nicholson's assurance of safety, Mr. Bray the master-mason carefully moved the stone at the SW angle of the chantry, when the following were revealed – matrix of "DE," followed by two lozenge-shaped stops one above the other both retaining the brass; then the matrix of "H", next to which we were rewarded by the discovery of a brass letter "E" *in situ*." So the mouse-hole may have been cut to facilitate loosening the stone underneath it, not to see the E.

According to Collinson, Haselshaw "made several useful statutes, some of which are observed to this day", and Watkin gives us several pages of examples from 1298, when Haselshaw was dean. Some resulted from "the custom of certain of the Vicars to leave the choir during Divine Service and to gossip with lay persons of doubtful reputation in the nave and behind pillars".

As if such gossiping vicars were not surprising enough, the statutes also attempt to control those who only attend the Office of the Dead on days when they will be paid extra for doing so, and they prohibit contact between a vicar and the mother of his children if he "has been convicted of keeping a concubine and having children by her", though this prohibition can be waived if they meet "in the presence of persons of good repute."

Haselshaw's slab is likely to be one of those referred to by Warner: "the large flat monumental stones, with their inscriptions defaced by the foot of the thoughtless passenger, only notify that *somebody* sleeps under them, whose importance, perchance, in the day when he flourished, seemed to promise he would not hastily be forgotten."

Walk now to the centre of the nave. On your right, in the central aisle, is a stone marked *Ina Rex*, in memory of King Ina of the West Saxons.

Ina is generally considered to be the founder of a collegiate church of St Andrew in Wells early in the 8th century (though the bishopric dates only from the 10th century and this cathedral from the 12th century). Britton makes no mention of this stone, assuring us that Ina, "having been shorn a monk, died in privacy in Rome between the years 725 and 740, and we have no account of his remains ever been having brought to England".

Reid explains that the stone "was placed here in 1917 on the supposed site of a large memorial known at one time to exist to the founder of the church, King Ina of the West Saxons who, however, was buried in Rome where he had become a monk. Under this stone was found a coffin, made for an ecclesiastic since a chalice was provided. This may well have belonged to Bishop Burnell, the first bishop to be buried in the nave."

Bishop Robert Burnell (1275-1292)

Dearmer calls Burnell "the greatest lawyer of his day", and Fuller says he was "by King Edward the First, preferred Bishop of Bath and Wells; and first treasurer, then chancellor, of England … He got great wealth, wherewith he enriched his kindred."

It seems that his conscience got the better of him, as Fuller continues: "to decline envy for his secular structures left to his heirs, he built for his successors the beautiful hall at Wells, the biggest room of any Bishop's Palace in England, pluck'd down by Sir John Gabos [Gates] (afterwards executed for treason) in the reign of King Edward the Sixth."

Gates had time to sell off the lead and timber before his execution (Mary objected to his support for Jane), and the weather has done the rest, but some walls of Burnell's hall can still be seen within the Bishop's Palace.

Now return to the north nave aisle, and continue into the north transept (where you will have watched the clock strike on your previous visit).

Dearmer summarises: "The Clock is a great favourite with visitors, who congregate in the north transept at the striking of the hour and laugh gently to one another when the quaint performance is over. 'Jack Blandiver' kicks his bell at each quarter in the most life-like manner, his feet trembling afterwards with the exertion; but at the hour, after Jack has sounded his four quarters, as the big bell begins to toll, the four 'knights' above the clock rush round in contrary directions, and charge each other with so much ferocity that one unfortunate is felled at each encounter, and has barely time to recover his upright position before he is again and again knocked down with a resounding clatter upon his horse's back. The other three fight twenty-four times a day unscathed."

Malden complains: "This clock attracts a very great number of visitors, some of whom seem to consider that there is nothing else worth seeing in the church and have a sadly inadequate sense of the respect for their surroundings. It is for this reason that a charge of 6d for admission to the quire is maintained" (in 1947), adding: "It is possible that in former days the relics of saints created a similar situation. At any rate the clock really is what it professes to be."

In fact the clock's mechanism was replaced in 1838 (and again in 1880), but the original is still operable, and is in the Science Museum in London.

The north transept also has an east aisle, which leads to the Chapter House steps. If you did not do so last time, you should *go to the doorway and look up those well-worn steps towards the Chapter House*, then turn to examine the three tombs distributed along the aisle.

| Bishop **Thomas Cornish** (died 1513) | The canopied tomb nearest the steps belongs to Thomas Cornish. Cornish had been a Suffragan (assistant or, in those days, substitute) bishop since 1493, under Bishops Fox, King and Hadrian de Castello. |

In Cornish's day the Bishops of Bath and Wells rarely visited Wells, so Cornish had the responsibility but not the authority.

Cornish's title was "Episcopus Tynensis" – Bishop of Tenos, Tyne or Tine - because, as Malden explains: "A bishop must be bishop *of* somewhere – if only in name. At one time bishops-suffragan took their titles from places which had been bishoprics but had been destroyed, usually by Mohammedan invasion."

In the Chapter Acts we read: "1509, Nov. 3.—Confirmation of a lease from the dean to Thomas Cornyssh, bishop of Tine and vicar of Wedmore, … of a pasture in the moor called Pulmede more, near his manor of Wedmore, with the fishery in the water along the breadth of the said moor … to hold to them and their assigns for 99 years. The lessees during the term must find a chaplain having a good voice with which he may serve God and Blessed Mary in Wedmore church, who shall swear on the gospels before the vicar that (by himself or another) he will celebrate low mass at St. Anne's altar in the said church thrice a week, namely, on Sundays, Wednesdays and Fridays, for the good estate of the said dean Cousyn and his successors and all his co-brethren while in the flesh and for their souls when they have departed from this light, and for the souls of Oliver, late bishop of Bath and Wells, and of deans Forest and Care [Carent], and of all parishioners of Wedmore."

Although many tombs have been moved away from the altar to make way for later burials, Cornish's tomb remains where he had asked to be buried: "near the entrance door into the chapter-house near the wall".

He seems confident of his reception on the other side, as he wills "that out of my goods my executors shall make full restitution and recompence to all who have been notoriously burdened and injured by me, if there are any such, which God forbid." He bequeathed cash sums to each of his executors and, to speed the process, offered 40 days indulgence to all who helped them!

Bishop Richard Kidder (1691-1703)	The elaborate monument next to Cornish's belongs to Richard Kidder. By the time of his death Kidder had written 122 pages of autobiography. Cassan quotes from them, and they were finally published in 1924, edited by Dean Robinson's wife Amy. It is in these pages that we learn of his tragedies: "I did … meet with another great affliction in the

death of all my children which were three" followed twelve years later by: "It pleased God that the small-pox first seized my eldest son, then my wife and my other three children. In less than three weeks I buried two sons and a daughter … Perhaps another man might have borne this much better than I could do."

The manner of his death was certainly a tragedy. Daniel Defoe, in *THE STORM: or, a collection of the most remarkable Casualties and Disasters which happen'd in the Late Dreadful Tempest, both by Sea and Land* (1704), gives an account by one Edith Conyers of Wells: "the dismal accident of our late bishop and lady was most remarkable; who was killed by the fall of two chimney stacks, which fell on the roof, and drove it in upon my lord's bed, forced it quite through the next floor down into the hall, and buried them both in the rubbish; and it is supposed my lord was getting up, for he was found some distance from my lady, who was found in her bed; but my lord had his morning gown on, so that it is supposed he was coming from the bed just as it fell."

Bath and Wells had fallen vacant in February 1690 when Bishop Ken was one of six bishops "deprived" for failing to take the oath of allegiance to King William III. Kidder declined the see of Peterborough, in part because "I knew very well I should be able to do less good if I came into a Bishopric void by deprivation", but in 1691 a letter from the Archbishop of Canterbury "let me know from the Queens direction that I was nominated to the Bishopric of Bath and Wells, and that the Earl said that I must not refuse it."

Kidder had not been the first choice for Bath and Wells, but Beveridge had already turned it down (and, perhaps because of this, he did not become a bishop for a further twelve years, eventually succeeding George Hooper at St. Asaph), so Kidder felt obliged to accept it.

To write "I have often repented of my accepting it, and looked on it as a great infelicity" while you are in office is the action of an unhappy man. He may have correctly assumed his words would not be published until after his death, but he must have really hated his move to Wells.

In the Preface to his autobiography Kidder writes: "The true reason for my writing these papers is this. I have bin greatly misrepresented by my Enemies, and by that meanes have bin deprived of the opportunity of doing the good I might otherwise have don, and Religion hath suffered by it." Robinson's biographical introduction adds: "Everything in which Kidder was concerned was unfortunate … We find it hard to judge him justly. It is he himself, by his perpetual self-justification, who makes it so hard."

Let's begin with Kidder's first preferment: "So it was that I was chosen, and Mr Attwood passed by to his great advantage, for soon after the Rectory of North Cadbury became void and fell to his share, which is of greater value and better aire by far." When he moved to London "I had not been many years at St. Martin Outreach before I was surprized with the gowt … I cannot express the tortures I endured" and, while there, enemies continued to appear, though "I am willing to forgett the great wrong was don me in a public print."

At Wells he is resented for having taken Bishop Ken's place, and then he finds fault with the Dean and Chapter: "These things were all agreed on but the Dean and Chapter never performed their part." Later he complains that "their design seems to be plainly to bring in their kindred and faction" and "my Enemies have found out a trick to avoid the trying of this cause."

Kidder devotes many pages to "the causeless troubles given me by Mr Samuel Hill Clerk and Rector of Kilmington", prompting Robinson to make an editorial note that Hill had previously been made a Prebendary by Bishop Ken and was subsequently appointed an Archdeacon by Bishop Hooper, so "we are inclined to suspect that there is another side to the story."

As if ecclesiastical life were not enough of a trial to a gout-ridden man, Kidder then suffered years of anxiety when one of his two daughters (evidently the only survivors among eight children) developed an on-off interest in a local doctor, the doctor blaming Kidder for the various "off" periods - sometimes justly, sometimes (says Kidder) unjustly.

Kidder's memorial was paid for by his daughter, Anne, who died a spinster. He does not tell us which daughter the doctor pursued, and even the monument does not tell us the name of Kidder's wife, but Turner says that the wife's name was Elizabeth, and adds that his other daughter, Susanna, married an early governor of North Carolina.

Bishop John Still (1593-1608)

Next to Kidder's monument is another enormous tomb which, Britton considers, "exhibits the uncouth heaviness in fashion in James the First's time." It belongs to John Still, who was appointed to this see and made Vice-Chancellor of Cambridge University in the same year.

Britton says: "This Prelate has long been reputed to be the author of 'Gammer Gurton's Needle' which, as Warton says, 'is held to be the first Comedy in our language; that is, the first play which was neither Mystery nor Morality, and which handled a comic story with some disposition of plot, and some discrimination of character'" but he then points out that the play was written and printed in 1551, at which time Still was just eight years old.

Harington had been Still's student at Cambridge, and his words on Still are contained in a document "written for the private use of Prince Henry", the elder son of James I (who would have been Henry IX had he not died before his father). Harington makes no mention of the story, even though we would expect such a prodigious claim to be made in this document, as it might inspire a young prince to develop his own talents.

Harington does speak well of Still, as you reasonably might of your old tutor, particularly during his lifetime: "I hold him a rare man for preaching, for arguing, for learning, for lyving", but he regrets being unable to get a clear answer on the question of witches. He was merely assured that we pray daily to be delivered from the devil because he is "as willing to have us thinke he can do too much, as to have us perswaded he doth nothing", leading him to conclude that "I could only wish that he would make lesse use of logique, and more of rhetoricke."

Fuller remarks on Still's abilities as a debater: "He was not less famous for a preacher than a disputant … he did not stick to warn such as he disputed with in their own arguments, to take heed to their answers, like a perfect fencer, that will tell aforehand in what button he will give his venue" and adds that he "gave five hundred pounds for the building of an alms-house in the city of Wells".

Now turn left into the north quire aisle.

There are some effigies of Saxon bishops on your right, but Reid says they were made for Bishop Jocelyn in the 13th century (when the See returned to Wells from Bath). Colchester says that when the bone boxes were opened in 1978 they were found to be jumbled, but a pathologist has sorted them to ensure that each box now contains the appropriate number of bones of each type, though whose they are is less certain.

Bishop Gilbert Berkeley (1560-1581)	After those comes what Reid calls "a rather clumsy chest tomb" with some letters of its inscription picked out in colour. This is the tomb of Gilbert Berkeley. Colchester says adding up the coloured letters as if they were Roman numerals gives the date of Berkeley's death.

Berkeley fell victim to Harington's pen: "he was a good justicer … saving that somtimes being ruled by his wife, by her importunitie he swarved from the rule of justice and sinceritie, especially in persecuting the kindred of Bourne his predecessor. The fame went that he dyed very rich, but the same importunate woman caryed it all away, that neither church nor the poore were the better for it." This particular comment prompts Fuller to qualify his general praise for Harington as a writer: "A posthume book of his is come forth, as an addition to bishop Godwin's Catalogue of Bishops; wherein (beside mistakes) some tart reflections on Uxoratos Episcopos might well have been spared."

Cassan describes Berkeley as the "First Protestant Bishop of Bath and Wells", but also expresses reservations: "He appears to have been an Adam at once in preferment, having commenced Bishop, without passing through the inferior grades, at least I find no record of such." Fuller's contribution is the impenetrable "He died of a lethargy, being eighty years of age."

Now look up and over the quire walls to see the clerestory windows.

Three look hardly worth a mention, as Colchester explains: "The design of the three westerly clerestory windows is very weak. This is not wholly the fault of the master mason. For cusps have been carelessly hacked off, perhaps with an axe, to simplify the re-glazing. This may have been during the period of the Commonwealth, when contrary to expectation, some of the windows were reglazed under the 'Preacher'", **Cornelius Burges**. The DNB tells us that "the protector and council agreed on a salary of £200 a year for his preaching twice every Sunday at the cathedral church of St Andrew in Wells" in 1656.

Wood details Burges's rise, and his fall: "Afterwards growing very rich, he purchased several lands, as the manor of Wells belonging to the bishop thereof, and the habitation of the dean there, which he mostly plucked down and rebuilt. And being so done he wrote a book to shew that there was no sacrilege or sin to alien or purchase the lands of bishops and chapters: which being taken into the hands of many curious readers, had the licentiousness of a second impression, an. 1659. But upon the king's restoration he lost all, having about an year before been offer'd twelve thousand and odd pounds for his house and lands at, and near, Wells; whereupon retiring to Watford in Hertfordshire before-mention'd, lived obscurely there, and died in a mean condition."

Dearmer describes the window behind you as "modern glass erected in honour of Bishop Ken, as a memorial to Dean Plumptre who died in 1891", though Colchester considers it "unsatisfactory as a coloured window because it is so overcrowded. That was the fault of Dean Plumptre, who commissioned it to celebrate Ken's bicentenary in 1885."

Bishop Thomas Ken (1685-1690) As you learned in Bishop Kidder's story, it was Thomas Ken who survived a moral quandary. Bishop Ken was the author of the Morning, Evening and Midnight Hymns, all three of which include the line "Praise God from whom all Blessings flow." These words are probably known to even more people than have heard of *The Compleat Angler*, whose author Izaak Walton was married to Ken's sister.

Anderdon's biography says Ken had already shown he was not a typical 17th century cleric: "It was inconsistent with Ken's views of the ministerial office to hold more than one living, though it was then a common custom."

Ken succeeded George Hooper as chaplain to Princess Mary (niece of Charles II', daughter of the future James II): "whose principles were thought to be in danger from the Presbyterian influence of her husband, William III of

Orange", (also her cousin: both were grandchildren of Charles I). "William was a hero in the field, but not an amiable master ... Ken soon perceived that he treated the young Princess with undeserved coldness and severity, insomuch that himself and others attributed her declining health to his unkind usage."

Ken seems to have annoyed William by speaking out on any issue which he considered incorrect (notably, says Dearmer, "by persuading Count Zulestein to marry a lady whom he had seduced"), so it is likely that this appointment in Holland was terminated by mutual agreement.

On his return he was made chaplain to Charles II, but Anderdon says his forthright views posed a problem when Charles brought Nell Gwyn to Winchester: "He absolutely refused her admittance, declaring that a woman of ill repute ought not to be endured in the house of a Clergyman, especially the King's Chaplain ... far from being offended, Charles appears to have admired the Christian boldness of his chaplain."

And so Ken kept his job as chaplain, and Dearmer mentions Charles's reputed comment on Bishop Mews's successor that "no-one should have the See but 'the little black fellow who refused his lodgings to poor Nelly'." Ken was consecrated Bishop of Bath and Wells in Charles's lifetime - though Charles died only a week later.

Ken was so attentive to Charles during his final illness that he found no time to complete the formalities of his appointment. Charles's brother, the Catholic James II, had to issue new instruments for the purpose, and Ken took office in 1685, the year of the Monmouth Rebellion. Dean Malden quotes the Chapter Book recording how "the fanatical rebels who this morning stole all its furniture, all-but destroyed the organ and turned the sacred building into a stable", and he speculates that this plundering may have been fatal to Monmouth's campaign.

Anderdon tells us that despite this, after the Battle of Sedgemoor, Bishop Ken "did not stop to consider if the King would resent his interference; but fearless in his mission of mercy he wrote to remonstrate against the cruelty of his officers.   Not content with this, he engaged with all his wonted zeal in alleviating the misery of the survivors. Some hundreds of the rebels being imprisoned in Wells, he daily relieved them in prison, and prayed with them."

Wood tells us: "King James II, who seemed to have a respect for him, usually said that Dr.Ken was the best preacher among the protestants", though even this did not secure the better treatment Ken had sought for the rebels.

Collinson describes Ken as "a zealous guardian of the Church against Popery", so when James issued his Declaration of Indulgence (granting some religious freedom to non-Anglicans) and called for it to be read in all churches, Wood says, of Ken: "On the 8th of June 1688, he with five other bishops (beside the Archbishop of Canterbury) were committed prisoners to the Tower of London for subscribing a petition to his majesty king James II wherein he and the rest '*shewed the great averseness that they found in themselves to the distributing and publishing in all their churches his majesty's late declaration for liberty of conscience,*' &c. where continuing till they were publicly tried for the same (being esteem'd a seditious libel against his majesty and his government) in Westminster hall, were to the great joy of the true sons of the church of England released thence on the 15th of the same month."

In that same week a son was born to James II's Roman Catholic second wife Mary. Fears of a Catholic dynasty in Britain led to an invasion by James's son-in-law-cum-nephew William of Orange.

The army and navy supported William (and his wife Mary, James's Protestant daughter by his first marriage - isn't it all complicated?), so James fled the country. Ken had not agreed with James's beliefs, but he had sworn allegiance to him as sovereign. He therefore felt unable to swear allegiance to a new sovereign, William III, while James II was alive (and had not abdicated, but merely fled).

Bishops who shared Ken's view again included the Archbishop of Canterbury. Such clergy were known as 'non-jurors'. Inevitably, Wood tells us, "About Candlemas in 1690 this worthy bishop Dr. Ken, who was esteem'd by many for his great charity, constant preaching, great devotion and obliging demeanor, was depriv'd of his bishoprick for not taking the oaths of allegiance and supremacy to king William and queen Mary."

Anderdon says that after William III's death in 1702, Ken's successor was offered another vacant bishopric, to allow Ken his old job back, but Ken refused: "The statement is that he objected to the oath of abjuration." This was the oath which all holders of public offices were then required to swear, renouncing the claims of James II's overthrown Stuart dynasty.

As you know, the vacancy created by Ken's dismissal was reluctantly filled by the unfortunate Richard Kidder, but Anderdon says Ken nearly suffered a similar fate on the night of the Great Storm, while staying in Wiltshire. Ken wrote to the Bishop of Norwich: "the workmen found that the beam which supported the roof over my head was shaken out to that degree that it had but half an inch hold, so it was a wonder it could hold together."

Ken later became chronically ill, and Anderdon quotes Hawkin as saying: "he had travelled for many years with his Shrowd in his portmantua, which he often said 'might be as soon wanted as any other of his habiliments'." His final journey was from Sherborne to Longleat where "his shroud was by himself put on by way of prevention, that his body might not be stripped." As his friend Hooper was still alive, Ken might have been buried here, but he asked to be buried "in the churchyard of the nearest parish within his diocese, under the east window of the Chancel, just at sun rising", so his grave is in Frome.

The same coat of arms is on the right of each of the next two windows.

The arms belong to Bishop Knight. One illustration surmounts the arms with a Bishop's mitre while the other has a Dean's cap. Three bishops had previously been Dean here, but Bishop Knight was not one of them, so it appears that the window has been changed.

Dean Richard Woleman (1529-1537)

The first window, opposite the quire's north entrance, commemorates Richard Woleman, though Wharton can find nothing to say about him. Britton says that Woleman and Bishop Knight erected a market house in Wells, which seems odd as Woleman was dead before Knight became bishop, but William Knight "Secretary to the King" was Woleman's executor and residuary legatee.

In his will Woleman asks to be buried in Westminster, and perhaps he was, for it would certainly help to explain why one of his bequests was "to every prison in London, viz., Newgate, Ludgate, the Benche and the Marshallse, 20s., praying those that be therein to say Dirige, or if they cannot 'De profundis,' of if they cannot say 'De profundis,' to say of their charytie such devotion as God shall put in their mynde."

Jewers suggests that Woleman's arms must be those in the left hand pane, so Colchester suggests that the right hand pane should display his successor's arms – and Woleman's successor was Thomas Cromwell.

Dean Thomas Cromwell (1537-1540)

Freeman disapproves of Cromwell as dean: "from 1537 to 1540, the Deanery was irregularly held by the King's favourite, Lord Cromwell, who, of course, as a layman, could not perform its duties". Wharton is more scathing: "pessimo exemplo tenuit. Capite plexus est 1540 28 Julii."

For those of us whose Latin is rather rusty, Hardy explains that "Thomas Cromwell, *earl of Essex*, held this deanery from 1537 to the time of his death, which happened at the block on Tower-hill, 28th July 1540." Sadly, he doesn't offer a translation of "pessimo exemplo tenuit".

Cromwell's major ecclesiastical achievement was urging the introduction of Coverdale's Great Bible into English churches. His political error came in advising Henry VIII to marry Anne of Cleves. She duly became Henry's fourth wife, but was later divorced, and on the day Henry married his fifth (Catherine Howard) Cromwell was beheaded.

Coincidentally, Cromwell's bishop (John Clerke) had died in mysterious circumstances after visiting the Duke of Cleves to discuss King Henry's divorce from Anne. We may reasonably assume, then, that 1540 ranks high among the difficult years in the history of the diocese.

On your right, opposite the undercroft entrance, is the effigy of a bishop.

Bishop
Bishop Ralph of Shrewsbury (1329-1363)

Ralph's election, in both Bath and Wells, caused a lot of trouble in Rome, as Cassan explains: "Pope John XXII claiming the provision, as it was called, of all vacant Sees, was indignant at the appointment of Ralph without his concurrence; but, in the end, the Bishop obtained the consent of the Pope, '*ingenti pecuniae summa*' says Walsingham, which Godwin has elegantly translated, '*with a huge sum of money*'."

Ralph proved to be a great success, for which Fuller gives two reasons: "this bishop is most memorable for erecting and endowing a spacious structure for the vicars-choral of his cathedral to inhabit together" and more generally: "He much ingratiated himself with the country people by disforesting Mendip; beef better pleasing the husbandman's palate than venison."

Ralph was one of the longest-serving bishops of Bath and Wells, and Britton tells us that "this prelate, in 1361, was excused from attending Parliament on account of his great age" (about 75). He bequeathed £40 in "penny-dole" to be distributed among the poor, but he was less generous to those less deserving: "I remit to the Abbot and convent of Salop £20 in which they are indebted to me" and "I bequeath to my Lord the King of England £100 owed to me by various debtors if he can cause the said money to be levied of the same debtors according to the information of my executors." It seems that Debt Recovery Agents are not a new invention!

Like those of many highly-esteemed bishops, Ralph's tomb was installed adjacent to the high altar but, like others since, his has been moved to make way for those of his successors.

Quite when the softness of the alabaster proved such an attractive material for scratching your initials on we don't know, but at some time between 1363 and Britton's first edition in 1824 the effigy became "much defaced with lettorial incisions, made by mischievous boys." Reid dates the names inscribed to the 17th century, but if you search carefully you will find dates as recent as 1809.

Look just beyond the next pillar at a floorslab dated 1690 and written in Latin to mark the burial place of "Johannes Sellek S.T.P."

John Selleck Archdeacon of Bath (1661-1690)

Davis says: "In the north aisle of the Choir is a plain stone to the memory of John Selleck, Archdeacon of Bath and Canon Residentiary. He was Ambassador of Charles II to the Algerines, to redeem the English prisoners from captivity." Colchester says there were 162 captives, and they had to be purchased from their individual masters. Remarkably, the total cost was exactly the £10,000 (subscribed by the English clergy) which Selleck and his colleague Canon John Bargrave of Canterbury took with them to Algiers in 1662.

Guy tells us that Selleck needed some luck to become canon residentiary because Charles II, once the monarchy had been restored, was deluged with petitions for preferments and was found to have recommended both Selleck and the new Archdeacon of Wells (Grindall Sheafe 1660-1680) for the same vacancy. At the time Sheafe should have had precedence, as Selleck was not yet an archdeacon, but Selleck's letter of recommendation had been issued two days earlier than had Sheafe's. "When asked, the king said Selleck was to be preferred, but Sheafe to be given the subsequent vacancy, which did not occur until 1664."

Beside Selleck's slab is one of the tombs made for those bishops whose remains were moved to this cathedral from the original Saxon one.

Britton considered that the effigy had a priest's cap rather than a mitre, but Reid says the mitre is authentically of the Saxon type.

Bishop Giso of Wells (1061- 1088)

Bishop Giso had a difficult start. Collinson says he had been Chaplain to Edward the Confessor, who banished the future king Harold from the kingdom when Harold's father Godwin raised an army against Edward in 1050. Because of this, Edward had bestowed all of Harold's estates in Somerset on the church of Wells, but Harold objected and "had, in a piratical manner, made a descent in these parts, raised contributions among his former tenants, spoiled the church of all its ornaments, driven away the Canons, invaded their possessions, and converted them to his own use", so it was in this state, Collinson says, that Giso found his bishopric.

Naturally he protested but (again from Collinson): "Bishop Giso in vain expostulated with the King on this outrageous usage; but received from the Queen, who was Harold's sister, the manors of Mark and Mudgley as a trifling compensation for the injuries which his bishoprick had sustained. Shortly after Harold was restored to King Edward's favour, and, made his captain general; upon which he in his turn procured the banishment of Giso, and when he came to the crown, resumed most of those estates of which he had been deprived."

Fortunately, Freeman is able to assure us "as is commonly the case with what we read in county histories and books of that class" much of Collinson's tale was invented, perhaps in previous centuries, or even by Collinson himself. "Gisa does not accuse Harold of taking anything which had ever belonged to the see, but only of hindering Duduc's will in favour of the see from taking effect … Gisa was never banished … Gisa himself adds that Harold, after his election to the Crown, promised to restore the two lordships and to make other gifts as well. This he was hindered from doing by what Gisa calls God's judgement upon him, that is to say, the Conquest of England."

Now look across the aisle to the Chapel of Corpus Christi in the north-east transept, and note the effigy on an altar tomb at the entrance.

Dean John Godelee (1305-1333)	John Godelee is the dean of bishop Drokensford's time, and Dearmer's praise is lavish: "Dean John de Godelee was the last great builder of the church of Wells. The power of the bishop in his own church is already declining, as that of the chapter rises, and it is the dean who now organises the works".

Dearmer excludes Ralph of Shrewsbury from this generalisation, as Ralph regained some control when he succeeded Drokensford.

Watkin's translation of Statutes from Godelee's time includes: "The clergy of the church of Wells are in the habit of instituting theatrical displays between the feast of Christmas and the Octave of Holy Innocents' Day, introducing dressed-up figures into the Church, there to exercise silly pranks and gesticulations. Since this is utterly opposed to clerical decency, hinders divine service and is forbidden by the Holy Canons, it must cease at once".

Dean Malden acknowledges Godelee as the third successive dean to make his mark on the fabric of the church, but adds an unexpected tale: "A malicious rumour states that the last-named was so much annoyed at his failure to get himself elected abbot of Glastonbury that he endeavoured to set fire to the 'moors,' as the peat-bogs which encircle it are called, with a view to destroying the house. We may hope that the story is without foundation. If the attempt were made, it was not successful."

Having cast doubt on Godelee himself, Malden does the same for Godelee's tomb: "This ascription appears to be no more than a modern guess, based on insufficient evidence. … The base may be dated about 1330, and it is therefore possible that it contains the body of Godelee. It would be natural for him to be buried close to the Lady Chapel in a position corresponding with that of Bishop Drokensford (1309-29) on the other side. But it appears to be impossible that the figure which surmounts it should be later than about 1270."

Reid is more positive, calling on a famous dean for support when he tells us: "Dean Robinson in 1925 thought he could read IC:JACET:MAGISTER:JOH. It can only be reported forty years later that four letters remain: IC:JA. There can be little doubt, however, but that this is the tomb of Godelee."

For all Dearmer's praise of Godelee, he believed that this tomb belonged to Dean John Forest (you will recall that Dean Forest had asked to be buried "before the great door", and that we have found no sign of his grave there). He states: "at the entrance to the little transept is the tomb of Dean Forrest (ob. 1446), similar to that of Drokensford in the opposite aisle, but more mutilated." In this belief Dearmer was agreeing with Davis, but Britton was more cautious: "an altar tomb, sustaining a recumbent effigy of a priest, said to perpetuate Dean Forest, who died in March 1446." Forest had been dean for eighteen years when Bekynton became bishop, and Wharton tells us that "huic senectute fracto quatuor Coadjutores ab episcopo dati sunt" a year later, so as a coadjutor is an assistant to a bishop we may assume that his health had been failing for some time.

Now step inside the Chapel of Corpus Christi, and look across to the far right hand corner where there is another effigy on an altar tomb.

Bishop Robert Creyghtone (1670-1672)

Although Creyghtone only became bishop shortly before his death, he was Treasurer of the diocese from 1633 until 1646, in which year, Cassan tells us: "Dr Creighton's loyalty endangered his person and property; and to save the former he joined the King's troops at Oxford, but he was afterwards obliged to make his escape into Cornwall, in the dress of a day-labourer, and embarked in order to join Charles II abroad, who employed him as his chaplain, and bestowed on him the Deanery of Wells, of which he took possession at the Restoration."

Creyghtone, as Dean, presented the cathedral with the brass lectern you can see behind you in the retroquire. Its inscription refers to exile for fifteen years, which is consistent with his return on the Restoration of the monarchy in 1660.

As Monmouth's rebels did not steal the lectern, the removal of the brass inlays from so many graves and tombs may reasonably be blamed on Reformers, or Oliver Cromwell's supporters.

Another Robert Creyghtone is associated with Wells just after this one. Guy uses Roman numerals to distinguish them, as in "Robert Creyghtone II, the precentor and a residentiary for sixty years (1674-1734) has a continuing reputation as a musician, some of whose chants and anthems long remained in the cathedral choir's repertoire." Some sources erroneously attribute this skill to the Treasurer/Dean/Bishop, but Guy says the musician was the bishop's son (and married Bishop Piers's grand-daughter).

Everyone seems agreed that Dean Creyghtone also paid for re-glazing the Great West Window, though the date for this is uncertain, Davis even offering the implausible "about the year 1647, with painted glass collected by him on the Continent, during his Exile with King Charles the II".

On your left as you leave the Chapel of Corpus Christi is the Chapel of St. Stephen, and on a floorslab to the right is a brass shield.

The shield commemorates our only Noble Dean, Lord Francis Seymour.

Dean Seymour (Lord Francis) (1766-1799)	Of Dean Seymour, Reid can tell us only that "In the first bay of the south walk was a charming medallion to Lord Francis Seymour, son of a Duke of Somerset, and Dean, who died in 1799. This recently [1963] fell and disappeared, but as a measure of reparation the Corporation of Wells has named one of its new roads 'Seymour Avenue'."

Guy, having recounted details of a dispute between Bishop Willes and Dean Creswicke, adds: "Under the aristocratic Lord Francis Seymour, life at the cathedral resumed a more placid course only interrupted in 1778 by the misconduct of Canon Robert Wilson, whom the chapter ordered to be 'sued and prosecuted' for 'his often brawling in the said cathedral church at the time of divine service and disturbing the same.'"

Now walk round the screen from St Stephen's into the Lady Chapel.

Dean Matthew Brailsford (1713-1733)	With its back against that screen is the largest money-box you are likely to have seen today - a huge wooden chest bound in iron. If you look carefully at the floorslab on which it stands, you should detect part of a Latin inscription. Jewers's copy includes the word "Matthaus", and the slab belongs to Dean Matthew Brailsford.

The name of Claver Morris may not yet be familiar to you, but Guy quotes from Morris's diary for 1718: "I regretted that the Solem Worship of God should be abased and ungracefully perform'd because the Dean thought himself not humble enough Bow'd to and reverenc'd". Dean Brailsford?

As you walk across the cathedral towards the south-east transept, you are walking through the retroquire. You will observe that virtually every paving stone is the floorslab of a grave, so we will rely on you to spot each of the following:

Adjacent to Brailsford, you will recognise Dean Goodenough's grave from Jewers's description of the "large slab, a long cross on steps, and under a canopy at the foot of the cross St. Andrew holding his cross, all brass".

Dean Edmund Goodenough (1831-1845)

Goodenough was dean when the Ecclesiastical Commissioners Act was passed: "The deanery of every cathedral shall henceforth be in the direct patronage of her Majesty [Victoria], who shall and may appoint a spiritual person to be dean, who shall thereupon be entitled to installation as dean of the church to which he may be so appointed."

The act must merely have formalised some aspects of the appointment system, because the first dean Hardy describes as "appointed by the King" was Bathurst back in 1670, while the last dean he describes as "elected" was Cosyn in 1498, though he agrees that on Goodenough's death "the deanery of Wells became vested in the Ecclesiastical Commissioners."

In 1842 Goodenough set up a fund for the restoration of the interior of the cathedral, and donated £500 to it himself (worth about £50,000 in 2015). Dearmer says that "In 1842 the restoration of the nave, transepts and Lady Chapel was commenced at the instance of Dean Goodenough, by Mr Benjamin Ferry. He removed the thick layers of whitewash which had been ingeniously applied to conceal the sculpture, and the long rows of marble tablets which had disfigured the aisles were shifted to the cloisters."

Britton tells us this fund raised £3,442 16s, which paid for the restoration of the nave, aisles and Lady Chapel and left a surplus (of £1241 9s 2d) for other work, which took place under his successor Richard Jenkyns, of whom you will hear more.

Goodenough's funding of re-glazing of the Lady Chapel's east window meets a mixed reception, for Dearmer considers "The eastern window was made up out of old pieces by Willement at Dean Goodenough's restoration, and its colour almost completely spoiled by modern insertions … the bad effect is mainly due to Willement's blue background".

In contrast, Malden observes: "The east window was 'restored' in 1843 by Mr. Willement at the private expense of Edmund Goodenough (Dean 1831-45), and it is only fair to say that the work could hardly have been done better."

In the centre of the retroquire, just in front of what Creighton's inscription calls 'this brazen Deske', or lectern, is a relatively plain slab.

Claver Morris MD	Morris is of interest partly because his early 18th century diaries have since been published as *The Diary of a West Country Physician*, the source of our only mention, above, of Dean Brailsford.

Morris also has an elaborate monument in the eastern cloisters, and when you reach it we will tell you much more about both him and his dealings with another person whose tomb you have already seen.

To prepare for your visit to Morris's monument, look towards the wall separating the retroquire from the quire and note that the central floor-slab also mentions Morris (though in Latin, on the grave of his infant daughter). The crest of lions and bulls on this slab appears in colour on his monument. Note also the new (well, newer) stonework in the central section of this wall, as we will be explaining this later.

At the corner of Morris's slab is a more elaborate one, inlaid with brass, with all the text in Latin and with no mention of the deceased's surname.

Bishop Richard Bagot (1845-1854)	"Ricardi Episcopi Bathon et Wellen" is Richard, Bishop of Bath and Wells, which has also been the title used by Bishops Kidder and Beadon, but the 1854 date identifies Bagot. Dearmer says Bagot came here "as a place of retirement after the worries he had gone through as Bishop of Oxford during the Tractarian movement."

Bagot's period of office coincides with that of Dean Jenkyns, who was busy dismantling the quire, but Dearmer leads us to suspect that, rather than suffering more worries over this, Bagot was a willing accomplice: "the palace, which had so wonderfully escaped the brutal adaptations of the eighteenth-century architect, was restored in 1846 by Mr Ferrey, and its west front completely altered … Bishop Bagot, at whose order the work was done, also rebuilt the kitchen and offices; in fact, he did what he could to destroy the unique character and beauty of a block of buildings without parallel anywhere."

In 1814 Davis mentioned "an ancient stone to the memory of Sir John Newton Bart." lying in the Lady Chapel, but Jewers could not locate it in 1892. The Latin inscription must have made it particularly intriguing:

Hoc non jacet corpus loco, Sed hic jacet pars pro toto

Davis's translation is: "Beneath a body find we not, But for the whole a part we've got." Newton died in 1661. In 1660 the corpse of Oliver Cromwell was exhumed for decapitation (his head is now buried at a secret location - reputedly the chapel of Sidney Sussex College in Cambridge), so perhaps this represented a similar secret.

At the head of the south quire aisle, separated from the Lady Chapel by an exotic canopied tomb with no inscription, is St John Baptist's Chapel. This must be Davis's "beautiful altar tomb, surmounted by an enriched canopy, supported by slender pillars, and ornamented with the most delicate sculpture, in pinnacles, crockets, trefoils, &c.", which he, Britton and Cassan believed was Bishop Drokensford.

Jewers had noted that the inscription said Drokensford, but suggested the tomb was for Canon John Marcel (died 1341). As you will see shortly, Jewers successfully used heraldry to identify Drokensford's tomb in the next chapel, despite its inscription to Bytton. The inscriptions on both tombs have since been adjusted.

Up against that exotic tomb, on the south side, is a white floorslab. It is commonly hidden by a noticeboard, or perhaps a vase of flowers.

Bishop George Henry Law (1824-1845)	This marks the grave of George Law, a bishop who was present at Queen Victoria's coronation. In 1829 he made a notable contribution to the parliamentary debate on the Catholic Emancipation Bill (for admitting Roman Catholics into the higher offices of state, and into the two Houses of Parliament). Britton details Law's reasons for objecting,

along with his assertion that "I have no other object in view, but to do my duty towards God and man: and I would rather go, as my great predecessor Bishop Ken did, to the Tower, than agree to sacrifice one tittle of our Protestant constitution in Church and State."

More practically "His Lordship introduced, on a large scale, the system of *Cottage Gardening*, and apportioned about one hundred acres of his demesne into small lots, from a quarter to half an acre to each individual, which he let to the poor at the same rent as to a farmer, for the cultivation of potatoes and vegetables. The 'Labourer's Friend Society' was established in this diocese."

Turn towards the south quire aisle, then walk towards the display of misericords (hinged seats from the quire, designed to provide support to those required to stand for long periods during services).

Bishop Richard Beadon (1802-1824)	Britton quotes from Beadon's obituary the suggestion that his responsibility (as Master of Jesus College, Cambridge, 1781-1789) for the then Duke of Gloucester "secured the royal favour, and paved the way to his subsequent high eminence in the church." By a curious coincidence, Beadon left Cambridge to become Bishop of Gloucester.

He died aged 87, but Cassan judges him harshly: "Bishop Beadon's advanced age, and the infirmities of nature, rendered him hardly competent for the last few years of his life, to the due administration of the affairs of this important See." Perhaps this was a nineteenth century case of blaming problems on the previous administration, as Cassan was writing a mere five years after Beadon's death, in the time of (and dedicating his book to) Beadon's successor Bishop Law, whose floorslab you have just seen.

Cassan presumably considers that Beadon's approach to patronage was still too conventional to merit a mention, but Greenhalgh details the appointment of Beadon's son as chancellor of the diocese, with another Beadon becoming the precentor, two more Beadons becoming canons, and two receiving prebends [see p.65]. Longevity seems to run in the Beadon blood, as one of his canon relations, Frederick, lived to be 101.

Now walk towards the south-east transept. It is currently known as St. Katherine's Chapel, but students of the various texts we have used as references will realise that most of these chapels have been renamed.

	The chapel is partly separated from the south quire aisle by an altar tomb with effigy, and the effigy is now clearly labelled John Drokensford.
Bishop John Drokensford (1309- 1329)	

Davis, Britton and Cassan all thought Drokensford was buried in the canopied tomb you recently passed, but Jewers knew better.

Jewers described this tomb in 1892: "An altar-tomb with an alabaster effigy of a bishop in his robes, recumbent, is inscribed Gulielmus Bytton, p'mus Episc' Bathon' et Wellens' MCCLXIX." He showed that the 'four swans heads' on the shields decorating the tomb were Drokensford's, not Bytton's. Clearly someone has since decided to correct this inscription (just as they deleted the Drokensford inscription on what is now believed to be Marcel's tomb) in the hope of avoiding future confusion.

Watkin discusses a number of documents from Drokensford's time which appear in the Cosyn Manuscript, and these suggest a man with a firm grasp on his authority, e.g. "Award of Bishop Drokensford in a dispute between John de Godelee Dean of Wells and William de Iatton the Subdean over the visitation of the Church of Woky annexed to the Subdeanery. The Bishop declares that jurisdiction over the Church of Woky belongs to himself."

Surprisingly (for an avowed anti-catholic) Cassan seems favourably impressed by Drokensford despite his sale of indulgences to fund building work, though he is less than keen on Godwin's account of Drokensford: "he improved the Bishopric with many noble buildings, and renewed and enlarged the privileges of the Church. He also, in 1325, was the cause of an indulgence of 40 days being granted to the contributors to the new works of the Cathedral. Godwin, solito de more [~ in his usual fashion], detracts from him, on account of nepotism, or providing for his nephews and kindred with the patronage of the diocese, than which, there certainly can be nothing more disgusting, but no assertions, that disparage a character, should be made in this random way. A list of the preferments, and the names of the kindred so preferred, should ever be annexed when nepotism is alleged."

Now look at the tomb on the back wall of this chapel.

<table>
<tr><td>

**Dean John
Gunthorpe
(1472-
1498)**

</td><td>

Gunthorpe's tomb is of interest for its early use of a gun in his arms, but his career in Wells is of greater interest for his impact on the Deanery building.

</td></tr>
</table>

Freeman regrets the modern windows but feels that it "still retains much of the dignity of design which it received from its builder, the learned Dean Gunthorpe." Dearmer considers the deanery "an almost perfect specimen of a fifteenth-century house, in spite of the modern sash windows and other alterations which deface it."

Davis proudly states that Gunthorpe "built the apartments next the garden, and had the honour to entertain King Henry VII, in his victorious return out of the West". Malden is happy to accept Davis's claim of the King's visit to Gunthorpe: "On Saturday, September 30th, 1497, Henry VII entered Wells at the head, it is said, of ten thousand troops (a figure it is difficult to credit) on his way to put down the rising of Perkin Warbeck ... The King had visited Wells more privately once before in the summer of 1491. He is believed to have stayed at the deanery on each occasion. As the Dean, John Gunthorpe, was an old and trusted servant this is not unlikely."

Dearmer describes Gunthorpe's tomb, then cautions: "Unless one has strong nerves, it is advisable not to look at the window." This may puzzle you, but he is complaining about the window "given by the students of the Theological College under Canon Pindar, its first Principal." Clearly others agreed, as it has since been replaced (in 1931, says Colchester).

In a deviation from the general praise for Gunthorpe's work on the Deanery, Davis reluctantly admits that "Cornelius Burgess, the despoiler of the Palace, fixing on the Deanery for his residence, considerably improved and repaired the same, about the year 1641."

In the middle of St Katherine's Chapel is the grave of the most notorious Dean of Wells in recent centuries: Richard Jenkyns.

In a departure from the general approach of this booklet we will defer much of our account of him until you are standing in the quire.

Freeman's comments will help to prepare you: "On the tomb of the doer of this havoc is written, with an unconscious sarcasm, 'Multum ei debet ecclesia Wellensis.'[~ The church of Wells owes him much]. The words seem happily borrowed from Lucan's address to Nero: "Multum Roma tamen debet civilibus armis" … Dean Jenkyns, however, did not employ fire."

The slab looks very dull when compared with the brass-inlaid slab chosen for Jenkyns's bishop (Bagot - back in the retroquire), but this seems not to be the monument which was the subject of Dearmer's uncomplimentary: "The middle of this unfortunate chapel is encumbered with a monument to Dean Jenkyns, the ornamentation of which may be taken as marking the lowest point to which the debasement of Gothic design has descended. A row of tiles round it serves to make it more conspicuous, and its unhappy prominence is further secured by a low brass railing of unutterably bad workmanship." The only clue we have to what he may have seen is given by Jewers, six years earlier: "Note. This is an ornamental cross, forming the top of a raised monumental slab, the first inscription being on the north side, the second being on the south side." Clearly it is now a far less striking tomb.

Before you leave this chapel, spare a moment for the brass plate on the west wall, in memory of Humphrey Willis. Davis thought it worthy of the only illustration in his 1814 edition. According to the popular translation, the final line (written in italics) tells us that the widow's relative "T.P." wishes for better things, though we must wonder whether that means better for the widow, or for T.P?

The translation shown nearby was made by the great-nephew of Samuel Taylor Coleridge. A lawyer rather than a poet, he had in the previous year spent three weeks cross-examining the Tichbourne Claimant.

Jewers confirms Coleridge's implication: "Thomas Popham became the second husband of Martha Willis, the widow of Humphry Willis", but Canon Church provides a relevant and intriguing extract from the Chapter Acts in 1606: "Humphrey Willis and Martha Drury submitted themselves to the Chapter for having procured matrimony in the Cathedral at an unlawful hour between eight and nine before noon without banns or licence."

Now walk back down the south quire aisle, and note the effigy of Duduc.

Bishop Duduc (1033-1060)	Duduc was Bishop of Wells from the time of King Canute to 1060, when Edward the Confessor was on the throne, so he must have seen the good and the bad sides of Edward's dispute with his successor Harold which, you will recall, proved inconvenient for Duduc's successor, Giso.

On the wall behind Duduc is a memorial tablet to the man responsible for correcting some of the excesses of Victorian Gothic restoration.

Dean Armitage Robinson (1911-1933)	Malden is certain of the good done by Robinson (his immediate predecessor as Dean): "Dr Robinson did a great deal for the fabric of the church in many ways, especially in the re-arranging of the glass in some of the windows: a difficult task, for which he had an unrivalled gift."

Indeed, in his discussion of Dean Jenkyns's involvement with the tomb a few feet to your left Malden says that "In 1922 what had been done (would it be too much to call it sacrilege?) was undone as far as possible, and tomb and chapel were 're-assembled' as they are now." Reid agrees, but for the date: "The canopy was happily rescued and restored by Dean Robinson in 1927."

Colchester's view, too, is generally complimentary. "His great scholarship, together with his energy in restoring to use the side chapels, repairing and discussing the ancient glass, and many other things, helped in some cases by the financial aid of wealthy friends, served to make this obscure cathedral better known." Despite this, he had reservations over Robinson's experimental cross for the rood, which was "a plain cross which did not seem to fit in well with the surrounding architecture. Sir Charles Nicholson, the architect, designed a new, more decorative one."

Colchester is also slightly critical of Robinson's work on the Saxon bishops' tombs (see p.12 and Giso p.19, Duduc p.31), which "were moved back to their present positions by Dean Armitage Robinson in 1913, when new wooden boxes were made for the bones and new stone boxes to hold the wooden

ones. In 1978 the contents of the boxes were examined by Dr Warwick
Rodwell, with the permission of the Dean and Chapter, and found to be in a very
confused state." You may rest assured, however, that "The bones were
sorted by the pathologist, Dr Juliet Rogers, so that each bishop now has the
correct number of limbs, and everything was carefully replaced."

*Beyond the next pillar, behind railings which make it part of the quire, is a
most unusual tomb.*

| Bishop Thomas Bekynton (1443-1465) | This is probably the most talked-about tomb in the cathedral. The skeleton below has been known to puzzle visitors, and we have heard "Is that his wife?" asked in earnest. Beckington's tomb is in the style known as "*memento mori*" (also "cadaver" or "transi"), resembling Archbishop Chichele's in Canterbury. |

This may be no coincidence, as Beckington succeeded to Bath and Wells
when John Stafford was translated to Canterbury to succeed Chichele.
According to Babington, Chichele placed the order for his tomb in 1425,
many years before he died: "On top there shall be a figure of myself as I am
in the eyes of the world, a great man, a great archbishop; beneath, a wasted
human frame, shorn of all its glory, wrapped about with a shroud, portraying my
sinful self in the eyes of God."

Britton tells us that "Beckington obtained such high repute for his learning that
he was employed at court to superintend the education of the young Henry the
Sixth." Cassan adds that he was author of "a well-timed treatise in
confutation of the Salique law of France. It was pleasing to Government, and
proved a passport to the author's preferment. The Salique law allows males only
to inherit." Under Salique law Henry VI's claim to the French throne was
invalid, as it derived from his mother, so this treatise would appeal to him.

Cassan adds the information that Beckington took unusual precautions
following the change of monarch (from Lancastrian Henry VI to Yorkist
Edward IV): "Perceiving himself sickly, and not likely to live long, Beckington
made his will; and fearing lest King Edward IV should nullify it, by picking

some quarrel of treason, as Godwin says, (a thing no doubt easy to be done, as the Bishop had always been a Lancastrian) he, with great cost, procured from the said King a confirmation of his will."

Freeman cites Godwin as his source for information about Beckington's will. "To his successor he gave 100l., upon condition he would accept it in lieu of all dilapidations, otherwise willing his executors to spend it in lawe against him." Fortunately, we can now read Bekynton's will for ourselves, and it turns out to be every bit as fascinating as Godwin had intimated. As we might expect from a man with a *memento mori* tomb, he willed "that my funeral expenses be moderate, that they shall be in the recreation and relief of the poor rather than in the solace of the rich and powerful."

Having done that, Bekynton gives the church of Wells £400 for twenty velvet and twenty damask copes to be made "so that the canons and vicars of my said church, when the occasion requires, may go in procession in one similar and uniform apparel, and not always in such diverse suits." He seems to have expected a dispute, for "if any of the canons residentiary of the said church, or any others, should demand any goods of mine in the name of a mortuary, or should make any impediment or disturbance as regards my burial" the whole lot goes to Winchester College Oxford instead!

It is Bekynton's predecessor, John Stafford, about whom he complains at length. "I had received nothing either in money or money's worth from my predecessor by cause of reparation, though, nevertheless, he is notoriously known to have received from the executors of Nicholas Bubwith of good memory, his predecessor, in money 1600 marks, and in other goods, such as mitres, jewels, and other precious things to the value of 1200 marks; and although my said predecessor left all and singular the manors and places belonging to my bishopric as though with no reparation done during the time, eighteen years, that he sat in this seat." But where is the famous threat to spend the money "in lawe"? Not in this version of the will, I fear.

Among Beckington's many benefactions to the city of Wells, Britton notes the right "to have and to hold, for ever, of the Bishop and his successors, one head for a water-conduit, with troughs, pipes, and other necessary engines above and under ground, to be supplied from a certain water within the precincts of our Palace, called St. Andrew's Well, by pipes of lead twelve inches in circumference." (i.e. about four inches in diameter.)

This was no one-sided bargain, as the citizens and burgesses were bound "'to visit, once every year, the spot in Wells Cathedral, where Bishop Thomas should be interred, and there pray for his soul and the souls of all the faithful deceased' for which service, the same prelate granted them an indulgence of forty days." We read that an indulgence is the "remission of punishment still due to sin after sacramental absolution." As the church set the penance in the first place, awarding an indulgence seems fair.

In his 1897 volume, Canon Church presents an anonymous report by "one who was present officially when, unhappily, this monument was moved, and the canopy over this altar taken down in 1849." The report described an investigation of Beckington's tomb: "a curiosity, entirely without irreverence, moving Dean Jenkyns to inspect it, under his orders an attempt was made, under my constant watchfulness, to reach the coffin and, with the Dean present, to remove the lid. The difficulty of carrying out this project was excessive, for the grave had been filled not with earth but with blocks of stone, strongly bound together with hard cement. On the discovery of this singular form of fortification the attempt was abandoned." This entire paragraph is missing from the 1909 edition, so perhaps it was deemed unpalatable.

Just past the south entrance to the quire is a floorslab set with brasses.

Bishop Arthur Lake (1616-1626) Fuller regards Bishop Lake as having "lived a real comment upon Saint Paul's character of a Bishop". He illustrates this claim with a large number of examples, notably: "such his austerity in diet (from university-commons to his dying day) that he generally fed but on one (and that no dainty) dish, and fasted four times a week from supper" and concludes that "This gracious Arthur … may pass for the first saint of his name."

Cassan says that Lake wrote his own 15-line Latin epitaph, which you might consider the fashion of the time, but instead he was given this brief inscription in English. His only consolation is his position behind the Cathedra – the Bishop's Seat which gives a Cathedral Church its title.

Adjacent to Lake's floorslab is a very imposing Victorian tomb.

Bishop Lord Arthur Charles Hervey (1869-1894)

Like his predecessor Eden, Hervey was a member of the temporal nobility. The tomb left Dearmer unimpressed and, as Eden lies in the Palm Churchyard, he hoped "that it is the last of its kind, for there is little room for more tombs".

Hervey is too modern to have been assessed by Cassan, so we have had to turn to the Oxford Dictionary of National Biography to discover that he was at Eton with Gladstone, and that forty years later Gladstone recommended him for the bishopric.

All of this might suggest that a title and influential friends were Hervey's only qualifications, but Colchester rates him the most outstanding bishop of modern times. He also observes that "so many young visitors stroke the lion cub at the bishop's feet with their sticky fingers that it has to be washed quite frequently" - though if the animal is from the Hervey family crest it's actually a snow leopard.

Across the aisle, and beyond Hervey's tomb is a badly worn floorslab most easily located from the adjacent slab for his wife, Abigail Hooper, which has been made from a far more suitable type of stone.

Bishop George Hooper (1704-1727)

Hooper arrived at Oxford the year after Thomas Ken, so Anderdon tells us that "the celebrated Dr Busby declared he was the best scholar, the finest gentleman, and would make the best bishop, that ever was educated at Westminster School", and that Bishop Ken and Dr Hooper were two of the clerics who officiated over the last hours of the Duke of Monmouth.

Although Hooper was translated here from St. Asaph, he had only just been made a bishop. During his time in the household of Princess Mary [niece of Charles II] in Holland: "One day, when he was chaplain at the Hague,

the Prince [the future William III] was talking to him about the great distractions
then in England, at the time of the Popish plot, and the great indulgence intended
to be showed to the Dissenters, but Hooper not expressing himself so favourable
to those measures as the Prince liked or expected, he said to him, 'Well, Dr.
Hooper, you will never be a Bishop'."

His first preferment came after William's death, under Queen Anne.
Anderdon gives us Ken's views on of Hooper in two letters written when
Hooper arrived at St. Asaph: "He is one of the best understandings I ever
knew, and if he will exert himself, will do excellent service to this sinking
Church …" and "He is of an excellent temper as well as understanding, and a
man of sincerity, though he may be of a different judgment (having taken the
oaths)" [i.e. he wasn't a non-juror - see p.15].

The following year Bishop Kidder was killed by the falling chimney we
mentioned on page 9, so "the Queen sent for Dr. Hooper, the new Bishop of
St. Asaph, told him the sad accident, and that she meant the Bishopric for him.
He expressed his thanks to Her Majesty, but begged to be excused, as he could
by no means eat the bread of so old a friend as Bishop Ken had been to him, and
entreated her Majesty's leave to propose to her the restoring him to his Bishopric
again. This the Queen highly approved of, and thanked the Bishop for putting
her in mind of it, and ordered him to propose it to Bishop Ken. … And now an
amicable contest arose between the two tried friends, each desiring the other to
take the See of Bath and Wells."

Ken famously continued to use his diocesan title until Hooper was
appointed, as Anderdon confirms: "I am informed that you have an offer of
Bath and Wells, and that you refused it, which I take very kindly, because I
know you did it on my account; but since I am well assured that the diocese
cannot be happy to that degree in any other hands than in your owne, I desire
YOU TO ACCEPT OF IT …. I told you long agoe at Bath how willing I was to
surrender my canonicall claime to a worthy person, but to none more willingly
than to yourselfe. … Dec. 6.   T. B. AND W." was followed two weeks later
by "I heartily congratulate the diocese of Bath and Wells of your translation, for
it was the good of the flock, and not my friendshippe for yourself, which made
me desire to see you in the pastorall chaire. … Dec. 20. T. K."

Now look to the right, past Abigail Hooper, to locate a raised slab against the wall, covered by a transparent plate.

Bishop William of Bitton II (1267-1274)

The raised slab belongs to William of Bitton (variously spelled Bytton, Button or Bucton). His uncle, also William of Bitton, had recently been bishop, so we call this one Bitton II. Freeman reminds us that "though being the kinsman of a bishop does not prove a man to be fit for high preferment, it does not prove him to be unfit", observing that William of Bitton II was "the holiest prelate of his time, and after his death miracles were held to be worked at his tomb", which is why we are puzzled that he was never nominated for canonisation.

Cassan says that "Matthew Paris informs us that so great was the fame of his piety, that Robert Kilwardby selected him ... to consecrate him Archbishop of Canterbury, in 1272; and his tomb was visited long after the Reformation, even till near Bishop Godwin's time, by the superstitious, especially by those who had the tooth-ache, but with what effect the reader must judge." The transparent cover suggests a persistent desire among visitors to touch the slab.

Dearmer even refers to him as "William Bytton (the Saint)", and records the account of a Mr J.R.Clayton, an eye-witness, that "on the coffin being opened in the presence of Dean Jenkyns it contained a skeleton in perfect order, every bone in its right place ... the teeth were absolutely perfect in number, shape and order, and without a trace of decay, and hardly any discolouration." Yes, the same Dean Jenkyns who tried to open Bekynton's tomb.

One unresolved puzzle is Hardy's description of Bitton's burial place "between two pillars on the south side of the choir, under a very sumptuous monument, with his effigies in full proportions habited in his pontificals."

The other mystery is why, a century after his death when the cathedral was in dire need of a Saint to raise revenue from pilgrims, they sought canonisation for a far less likely candidate, as you will learn on page 49.

On your left at the end of the corridor you will see an alabaster effigy.

Bishop John Harewell (1367-1386)	Davis explains: "at his feet are two hares, in allusion to his name", while Britton quotes Godwin's view that "this figure, which is of alabaster … represents the deceased as of a very fat and large form." Cassan also quotes from Godwin, saying that "Edward, surnamed the Black Prince, obtained then of the Pope this Bishoprick, for John Harewell, a chaplain of his."

The bequests in Harewell's will include "my larger gilt chalice wherever it be" to the high altar of Wells cathedral, and "To Jonetta daughter of Roger de Harewell my brother to her marriage 100 marks, this only because in this last year I gave her father 200 marks for the same purpose." Less grudgingly, he also gave each of his servants a year's salary in cash.

Harewell was bishop in the 14th century, like Bishop Ralph, whose badly-scratched likeness you saw in the north quire aisle, so it is no surprise to see that this alabaster has suffered in exactly the same way.

Cassan says the tomb is "now much defaced, I suppose by what Godwin calls the 'Sacrilegious Cormorants'." Godwin uses that phrase to describe those who appropriated the lands and revenues of the Deanery from Dean Fitz-something in 1547 (see page 83); this would have been Bishop Barlow's time but, as you read earlier, Barlow may not be entirely to blame. Indeed, it seems that even Archbishop Cranmer disposed of assets at that time to save them from those same Cormorants. The general damage may date from then, but we have noted graffitti with a date range from 1643 to 1843, the latter fifteen years after Cassan's book.

Dean Walter Medeford (1413-1423)	What you will not see nearby is the grave of Walter Medeford. We had hoped to find it because his will (in the same volume as Harewell's) asks for "My body to be buried, if I die in England, in the cathedral church of S. Andrew of Wells near the tomb of lord John Harewell of good memory, formerly Bishop of Wells", but it seems that his

bequest to the church of a mere £10 did not achieve this object. Evidently he expected a good turn-out for his obsequies and mass, as he also left "100s to be distributed by my executors to poor and needy persons coming of their devotion to the said church on the said day so that each may have 1*d* so long as the said sum shall last." His concern for his soul extends to bequests to "seven innocent women" and "ten virgins" if they will pray for him, and a great deal of money (£46) to "an honest priest" to continue doing so for seven years at a church in East Hagbourne.

Lots of persuasive bequests go to that church, enforced by the threat that these bequest are conditional on the church's vicar and parishioners allowing the priest to go about his duties. Otherwise they lose the lot to Bibury! Finally, a family squabble surfaces in his bequest to "Alice Hunt my sister £10 under this condition that she demand nothing from the legacies left to her in the will of Richard Medford, lately Bishop of Sarum, because as God is my witness the whole has been paid to her or to Robert Hunt my nephew, her son and her daughters."

At the end of the south quire aisle, walk back to the centre of the cathedral by going under the nearest 'scissor arch', then turn right again into the quire (sometimes choir). The OED helpfully explains that the choir spelling was introduced in the 17th century by analogy with chorus.

A prominent notice on your right as you enter the quire tells a version of the terrible tale of Walter Ralegh (no, not Sir Walter, but his nephew) and how he was "buried under the Dean's Stall by Mr Standish, a priest vicar, who was accordingly put in prison where he died."

Dean Walter Ralegh (1642-1646)	Malden, using "the words of a contemporary historian", tells us how Ralegh "was buried by Standish, one of the priest-vicars, who read the church service over his body, a crime for which he was imprisoned till the day of his death". Note the change of emphasis, suggesting the imprisonment was for reading the burial service, not for performing the burial.

In Wood's version the whole emphasis is on Ralegh: "on the breaking out of the rebellion … he was persecuted, plunder'd, and forced to abscond for his loyalty to his prince. At length being taken prisoner at Bridgwater by the rebels 21 Jul. 1645, he was sent to Banwell house as a captive, and after several removes to his own at Wells, where being committed to the custody of a shoe-maker (David Barret a constable of that city) by the committee of the county of Somerset, was treated by him far beneath his quality and function."

Having set the scene, Wood goes on to assure us that "the keeper thrust his sword into his groyn, shedding his blood as the blood of a dog; of which wound he died about six weeks after to the great grief of the loyal party."

Standish does receive a mention from Wood: "One Standish a clergy vicar of that cathedral was afterwards questioned by the aforesaid committee for burying him in the church; and his death being soon after call'd into question at an assize or sessions, there was a jury of rebels that brought in his murder either Ignoramus, or at least but man-slaughter; for they said that the doctor to shun the keeper's reading of a letter which he wrote to his wife, ran upon the keeper's sword, &c. Much about that time the committee turned the doctor's wife and children out of doors, and his son (as 'tis said) was forced to fly the country, for that he would have farther prosecuted the law against the murderer of his father."

Perhaps this variety of tales is why a recent book by Fiona McCall (*Baal's Priests*) pours cold water on the whole legend, particularly "the easily disproved claim by Long that Francis Standish, vicar of Wells, was imprisoned 'till the hour of his death' for burying Raleigh using the Prayer Book."

How easily disproved? Well, the Chapter Acts say "1634, Oct. 25.—Francis Standish appointed a perpetual vicar-choral", which sounds like the right man, so we assume Ms McCall has also looked at "1664, April 1 … The following vicars-choral appeared … Francis Standish …Thomas Standish".

We have included this mention of Thomas Standish because "1664, July 7–Thomas Standish, clerk, one of the vicars-choral, excommunicated for not appearing on the first day of this chapter, with the other vicars-choral …" The moral seems to be "Don't mess with the Dean and Chapter", so we wouldn't dream of suggesting that the notice should be changed!

The 1987 Colchester ends Ralegh's term in 1644, despite describing his death in 1646. The explanation may lie in another extract from the Wells

Chapter Acts: "1644–5, Jan. 28 [remember that New Year's Day was Lady Day, March 25th, until 1752] — It is this day ordered by consent of the persons heere present, that yf it shall heareafter happen that the corporacion of the deane and chapter to be dissolved by act of parliament or by any other lawful meanes ..." This suggest that the writing was on the wall for Ralegh and, as the next entry is dated 1660, this may be when he was "forced to abscond".

Now walk further into the quire, and seek a floorslab in the second bay, in the middle of the aisle.

| Bishop Jocelyn of Wells (1206-1242) | Jocelyn was forced into exile in 1208 for his involvement in the interdiction of the nation and excommunication of King John. This followed John's rejection of the Pope's choice - Stephen Langton - for Archbishop of Canterbury. The Pope lifted the interdict in 1213, but Colchester says that King John failed to honour his pledge to repay the five |

years' cathedral receipts.

Jocelyn had taken office as Bishop of Bath and Glastonbury, but Fuller says that "the monks of Glastonbury, being very desirous to be only subjected to their own abbot, purchased their exemption, by parting with four fair manors to the see of Wells", so in 1218 Jocelyn became Bishop of Bath.

Malden speculates, with the benefit of hindsight, that "If they had lost, it is possible that their house would not be a ruin to-day, as they would have had at least one powerful friend when the storm came."

Colchester says Jocelyn had asked the Pope for the "Bishop of Bath" title to be extended to "and Wells", but nothing happened because the Bishop of Norwich (who was the papal legate) did not answer the Pope's letter asking whether Wells had ever had a cathedral. Cassan disagrees on this point, as he refers to a Papal bull in 1218 enabling Jocelyn to resume the title Bishop of Bath and Wells.

Jocelyn was responsible for enlarging the quire, which is why he is buried at its centre. All we can see now is a plain floorslab, but Britton translates the Latin text in Leyland's 16th century "Itinerary" as: "Bishop Joceline was buried in the middle of the choir, under a marble tomb inlaid with his figure in brass."

Fuller, writing of Jocelyn in 1662 (after the Civil War but before the Duke of Monmouth), considered that "The Church of Wells was the master-piece of his works, not so much repaired as re-built by him; and well might he therein have been afforded a quiet repose. And yet some have plundered his tomb of his effigies in brasse, being so rudely rent off, it hath not onely defaced his monument, but even hazarded the ruin thereof."

Britton likewise expresses surprise, both at the plunderers and at unspecified 'restorers' : "So little respect, indeed, have the successive conservators of this fabric shewn to the memory of one to whom they are so much indebted, that they have suffered his monument to be utterly destroyed."

The destruction, however caused, was so thorough that, says Dearmer: "all traces of the burying-place were lost until, in 1874, an ancient freestone coffin was found under the pavement in the midst of the choir. Its covering stone had been broken, and the bones within disturbed; but on its discovery the stone was renewed, and the inscription *Jocelinus de Welles, Ep. 1242* cut on it."

While you are in the quire, look at the inscription on the pulpit.

| Dean Richard Jenkyns (1845- 1854) | If your Latin is a little rusty you might reasonably assume this was a monument to Dean Jenkyns and his wife, but you will be able to read the date 1853, and Jewers tells us that Jenkyns did not die until 1854 (his wife Troth died in 1857). Greenhalgh explains: "the stone pulpit was given by them at a cost of £200." We cannot blame Dean Jenkyns for |

what happened to Jocelyn's tomb, but clearly the architect (Anthony Salvin - presumably the A.S. in the inscription) needed to make drastic changes to fit this pulpit in (as it's not visible in the 1824 engraving).

Dean Jenkyns must be the first Crown appointment to that position (see Goodenough, p.24), so perhaps it was his 'day job' as Master of Balliol that secured the position for him.   He continued Dean Goodenough's restoration work, but found that remaining funds were insufficient.

Britton quotes from Jenkyns's 1847 appeal for more funds, which was launched "on account of the inadequacy of the fund to complete that part of the edifice which requires more than simple repair or restoration … viz. the *Choir*."

This, Jenkyns suggested, would cost £6,000, and he assured potential donors that his object was to "continue the great work of restoring to its ancient magnificence a great monument of the piety and architectural taste of former ages", which sounds as if he intends *only* repair and restoration – but the conflict between these statements was to prove significant.

Canon Church says, with restraint: "a reconstruction of the choir was made with a zeal not always according to later knowledge".   Dearmer is more explicit: "The restoration of the choir by Mr Salvin, which lasted from 1848 to 1854, was unfortunately of a less blameless character. … We need not dwell on the result; few restorations are more marked with the complacent ignorance of that strange time. … No real improvement in the choir of Wells is now possible till every trace of Dean Jenkyns' restoration is swept away; but, alas! what he destroyed can never be recovered."

Just what was done?   Dean Malden provides more details: "Jenkyns removed the old wooden stalls, which had seats above them for the families of the dignitaries, and replaced them with the present stone ones. … There are not now sufficient stalls if all of the prebendaries were present."

Had Dean Goodenough lived, he might have made similar changes, but we know from Britton's 1847 edition that he did not, and Canon Church says that "Those who saw the choir … in 1848, record that it presented an unusual amount of colour. 'The throne of the bishop was entirely painted over to represent green marble; on the panel at the back was a rude representation of a landscape. This paint, being in oil, was extremely tenacious, and gave much trouble in removal, and the effect produced by the change was extraordinary. The stalls and the panelling over them …were coloured. The pulpit was draped with crimson; the reredos, or wall behind the altar, was draped; the pew sides and bench ends, and altar rails, and sounding-board to the pulpit were of dark oak, a great contrast to the white stone which has succeeded.'"

Now return to the south transept, and walk to the second column down the south nave aisle. On your right is a chantry chapel, balancing Bubwith's on the opposite side of the nave.

Treasurer Hugh Sugar (1460-1489)

This chapel was built for Canon Hugh Sugar, but Davis called it "Bishop Beckington's Chapel" because Sugar was one of Beckington's executors. Colchester says it was built by Sugar's executors so it is called Sugar's chantry.

Sugar ("alias Norris", says Hardy) was appointed Archdeacon of Bath in 1459 but relinquished that to become Treasurer, a post he held for nearly 30 years. He is known primarily for this chantry and for his involvement in the repairing of the Vicars' Close.

In case you wondered what a Treasurer does, Watkin gives us William of Bytton (II)'s 1278 version of the duties, and they go beyond the purely financial: "To the Treasurer belongs the duty of cleaning the church when necessary ... He must also wash the vestments ... he is to provide reed mats ... He is to lay down new mats every year of the highest grade in the choir at Evensong on the Eve of St Andrew; not every year however before the High Altar, in the chapter-house or before the other altars: but only when necessary."

Britton tells us this is not the first chantry in this location, but that it is built "entirely of freestone, in place of a chapel of wood that previously stood there." Dearmer was not impressed by this substitution, saying that "before its erection, the altar of St. Edmund of Canterbury, who was canonised in 1246, stood here; and perhaps, when it comes to be used again, it will be maintained in honour of that most attractive scholar saint."

Reid explains that "On June 22nd 1489 Canon William Bocat, one of the executors of Treasurer Sugar, prayed for leave to take down and remove the wooden chapel (presumably housing the altar of St Edmund) and to rebuild the same." According to Malden, the wooden chapel was 200 years old because "the altar is said to have been erected in the year 1269. Ralph Erghum (Bishop 1388-1400) founded a chantry in the chapel and is buried there."

Dearmer is able to demonstrate the chantry's association with Sugar, as it bears "the initials H.S. and Sugar's arms, originally a 'canting coat', three sugar-loaves, and in chief a doctor's cap. Sugar's initials and arms also occur under the canopy."

Davis tells us that Beckington "bestowed a great part of his estate on the Vicars Choral, to repair their Close. This bequest was vested in his three executors, Richard Swan, Hugh Sugar and John Pope". Freeman gives Godwin as his source for the assurance that "The Bishops goods that remained unbequeathed, they bestowed for the most part, in building the Vicars close at Welles, which had beene begun by Bishop Ralfe long before; a sumptuous and beautifull worke."

Colchester is also conscious of the three executors' involvement with the Vicars' Close when he observes that "On the chimneys are plaques bearing the arms of the see of Bath and Wells alternately with Bekynton's personal arms. Below them are the arms successively of the bishop's three executors: Hugh Sugar, Richard Swan and John Pope (or Talbot). Bekynton bequeathed the residue of his estate 'for some charitable purpose, such as the repair of roads and bridges or the relief of the poor, or as my executors may see fit.' The executors saw fit to give high chimneys for the poor vicars, and once again the poor old Somerset roads and bridges went by the board."

Using someone else's money to build something, then having your own arms carved on it, is an intriguing idea, but evidently Sugar saw nothing wrong. It's equally intriguing to speculate where Colchester found this mention of roads, as it's certainly not in Weaver's edition of Bekynton's will. Perhaps he was thinking of the bequest of 1000 marks by Bishop Bubwith (see page 3).

Returning to Sugar's Chantry, Cassan quotes Godwin saying that Sugar, and Beckington's two other executors, "(as I have been told by old men,) lye buried in a ranke together, over against the great pulpit, under three marble stones of one fashion." If that is true, they must now be under the wooden stage which stretches between the two chantries.

If they are all buried here, it just shows how little notice was taken of the wishes of the departed: in 1475 Pope asked to be buried at St. Gregory in London (next to the old St. Paul's Cathedral), and made Swan one of his own executors. Swan went next, in 1486, wrote his will in English, and asked to be buried in "the chapel of the Blessed Mary next the cloister", which sounds like Stillington's chapel. Even Sugar himself wasn't sure where to be buried, dithering between the nave at Wells "before the cross there, made, fabricated and erected at my costs and expense", or before the altar of St Andrew in the monastery at Glastonbury "according as it shall please the Most High for me to die". Perhaps someone dug them all up and buried them together ... or perhaps Godwin was misinformed.

Now look at the pulpit, added to the chantry a century later for use as the tomb of William Knight.

| Bishop William Knight (1541-1547) | Fuller describes the circumstances of Knight's appointment by Henry VIII: "He was the first person employed to the Pope, to motion to him the matter of his divorce, advertizing the King, by his weekly dispatches, how slowly his cause (though spurred with English gold) crept on in the Court of Rome. After his return, the King rewarded his industry, fidelity, and ability, with bestowing |

the Bishoprick of Bath and Wells upon him."

Knight seems to have paid for the pulpit, even though he didn't know what he was spending his money on, as he wills his body "to be buryed within the cathedral church of Wells and for the chargis of my burial, bringing down of my corps and making of my tumbe, £100."

Shakespeare may be the most famous bequeather of second-best beds, but Knight wills away no fewer than four "fetherbeds", along with three bolsters. Like Bubwith (though on a far more modest scale), Knight was concerned about the state of the county's roads, leaving £20 for "the repair of highways about Bridgewater", which even he couldn't spell.

Most intriguingly he leaves £10 per year, for ten years, to pay "a preest to singe for my soule in the cathedral church of Wells" on at least four days a week, and "if Mr. Edon, my chaplen, after his return from his trouble, be not provided with a benefice by me I will he have the said service."

Colchester says that the pulpit inscription initially used Coverdale's 1539 text (Coverdale had been commissioned by Thomas Cromwell to provide a bible in the English language), but the King James Authorised Version of 1611 introduced a number of differences in wording. It was easy enough to change 'IMPROVE' into 'REPROVE', as you can see, but the rest of the text remains Coverdale's.

Near the pulpit is a large floorslab which may belong to Ralph Erghum, the last 14th century bishop; the other possibility is that it might be John Free from 1465 (you will read about him on the next page).

Bishop Ralph Erghum (1388-1400)	"In 1389, this Prelate obtained a grant of all the lead mines within his diocese, including the rich veins of the Mendip Hills" is all we really know of him from our reference books.

Fortunately we know from his will that he wanted to be buried "in the body of the church in the place where I have placed my stone near the altar of S. Edmund, Archbishop."

Erghum is another who uses his will to right perceived wrongs after his lifetime, with bequests such as "To Ralph Erghum, my nephew, the letters of obligation in which he is bound to me and the sums therein contained if he does not pay them to me before my death" and "To Thomas Cosyn the volume of Civil Law which he now has, lent to him by me on condition that he return to my executors all other books so lent to him".

Some uncertainty arises from Britton's assurance that Erghum's floorslab in the nave "on the west side of the chapel erected by Bishop Beckington's executor, has been inlaid with a brass episcopal figure, and two shields, as may be traced by the indents". Although this sounds a bit like the one you are looking at, the number of shields is wrong.

Similarly the lack of an inscription means this doesn't fit Dearmer's "on the west side of Sugar's chapel, another slab bears the inscription 'Radulphus Erghum Ep. 1401'". As Reid says Erghum's slab is much flaked and partly covered by the pulpit, it's beginning to look as if this is someone else's.

Only Colchester gives us a description of this slab: "the blue lias slab with the indents of a brass of a priest, with a long inscription below, four heraldic shields, and another inscription round the edge of the slab, with roundels at each corner, which presumably held the emblems of the Four Evangelists. Legend, backed by several eighteenth-century writers, says that this covered the grave of John Free." Why, though, might this John Free merit burial here?

| Bishop John Free (1465) | Collinson says "John Phreas, or Free, master of Baliol college in Oxford was elected to this see. He was born in London, and educated at the university of Oxford, where he acquired great skill in the languages of Greece and Rome. Thence he travelled into foreign parts with a view of inspecting their universities. In his |

course he practiced physick … and at length arriving in Rome, became acquainted with the most eminent literati of that city, who introduced him to Pope Paul II, by which means he acceded to this bishoprick; but did not enjoy it long, being poisoned at Rome a month after his appointment."

This "poisoned" may be an example of Collinson embellishing his sources, because the Canon of Wells merely says: "non sine veneni suspicione [~ not without suspicion of poison]", though Fuller is more definite: "poisoned (as is vehemently suspected) by some who maligned his merit." Colchester, rather more prosaically, says that "within a month, and before his consecration, he had died of food poisoning at the age of 35."

Unusually for Collinson, he does not mention Free's burial place, but he is clear that the appointment followed Beckington's death in "January 1464" and that Free's demise brought Stillington to the title of Bishop of Bath and Wells, if not actually to Wells.

Now go back to the south transept and look into the Chapel of St. Calixtus (Reserved for private prayer).

| Dean Henry Husee (1302-1305) | The exotic tomb to the right is now labelled with the name of Thomas Boleyn, but Jewers's survey identifies it as Dean Henry Husee. Wharton says: "Cantariam is insignem in Ecclesia Wellensi fundavit" of Husee. "Cantarium" can mean chantry, which will help to explain why this tomb has been linked with him. |

Our 19th century authors are all satisfied that it is Husee, but Malden is unconvinced, mentioning "a tomb which bears the name of Henry Husee (Dean 1302-5). This inscription is probably erroneous, the real occupant is believed to be Thomas Boleyn (precentor)."

Fashionable though that view may now be, Colchester was dismissive in 1987, saying "it is neither of Dean Husee nor of Thomas Boleyn, both of whom have had the tomb ascribed to them at one time or another", but he does refer to "St Calixtus's chapel, where Husee's chantry was", supporting Wharton.

Now turn towards the south wall, and examine the canopied tomb under the centre window (not the left window) of this south transept.

| Bishop William of March (1293-1302) | The only positive comment we have found is Britton's quotation from The Canon of Wells: "At his tomb were many miracles performed." Miracles mean saints, and the tomb of a saint attracts pilgrims; and revenue. Dearmer confirms that "Two unsuccessful efforts were made to obtain his canonisation". These attempts may have failed because William of March had been Edward I's Treasurer. |

Cassan quotes Godwin as having seen in "the records of our Church of Wells, the copies of divers letters unto the Pope and Cardinals, from the King, from divers of the nobility and the clergy of that Church, commending this man so for his holiness, testified, as they write, by many miracles; as they entreated very earnestly for his canonization."

So far so good, but Godwin admits: "I marvel much at it; for Matthew of Westminster and Polydore Virgil complain grievously of him, as the author of a heinous sacrilege, in causing the King to spoil all the churches and monasteries in England of such plate and money as lay hoarded up in them, for the payment of his soldiers." He then enters the realms of speculation with "such a fault stamped upon him, (how undeservedly soever) might bar him out of the Pope's calendar, who, otherwise, was not wont to be over dainty in affording that kind of honour, where fees might be readily paid for it."

This slight on papal integrity was too much even for the fervent protestant Cassan: "We may imagine Popes capable of such things ... but a suspicion of guilt, however strong, warrants not a specific charge of it."

To the right of this tomb are three doors. The third is a huge door to the cloister which has a small one set into it. Pull the handle and go through into the east cloister, down the steps, and walk forwards as far as an opening on the left. Go through this gap into the open air to what is called the 'Camery' (the OED defines camery as a disease of horses!)

Somewhere within the exposed foundations on the ground in front of you was once "the chapel of the Blessed Mary next the cloister", where one of Bishop Bekynton's executors had asked to be buried. It was built for Bekynton's successor, Robert Stillington.

Bishop Robert Stillington (1466-1491)	Stillington had been Lord High Chancellor of England from 1468 to 1473 and it seems being merely Bishop of Bath and Wells was too tame for him. Davis is no fan of his: "By deserting his sacred office, and interfering with political affairs, he incurred disgrace, and was imprisoned at Windsor, where he died."

The "deserting" is clarified by Colchester, who says Stillington visited the diocese "for only 3½ weeks in the whole of his tenure of the see for 25 years."

Similarly, the "interfering with political affairs" is explained by Cassan's transcription from Godwin: "With King Henry VII he sorted not so well; for the year 1487, about the time that Stokefielde was fought, in which Lambert [Simnel] was apprehended, (the counterfeit Earle of Warwicke,) I find that this Bishop was accused of treason, for yielding, (as we may suppose) some assistance unto the said Lambert."

Neither Fuller nor Wood mention Stillington, but in Clements Markham's 1906 book *Richard III - His Life and Character* we learn of Stillington's most famous political act, as we are told that "Dr Robert Stillington, Bishop of Bath and Wells, revealed to the Council the long-concealed fact that Edward IV was contracted to the Lady Eleanor Butler .... Dr Stillington thus becomes a very important personage in the history of King Richard's accession."

Edward IV had just died. This revelation makes his son Edward V illegitimate and Richard III the rightful heir (with no reason to murder those Princes in the Tower). Support for Richard was not likely to endear Stillington to Henry VII, so assisting Lambert Simnel was ... injudicious.

Stillington died in Windsor, but his body was sent for burial in his chapel at Wells, and Godwin continues the story: "In that chapel his body rested but a short time. For it is reported that divers old men who, in their youth, had not only seen the celebration of his funeral, but also the building of his tomb, chapel, and all; did also see tomb and chapel destroyed, and the bones of the Bishop that built them turned out of the lead in which they were there interred."

Stillington had been "buried in a beautiful chapel he had himself built in the cloisters, at Wells, which chapel was afterwards pulled down by Sir John Gates ... His body was disinterred for the sake of selling the lead in which it was deposited" says Cassan. Harington provides a more graphic description: "such was their thirst after lead that they tooke the dead bodies of bishops out of their leaden coffins, and cast abroad the carkases skarce thoroughly putrified."

Freeman explains that the suppression of chantries (where masses were said for souls, as in Stillington's chapel) in 1547 necessarily followed the change of doctrine after Henry VIII's break with the Church of Rome. Canon Church explains that "when the chantries were abolished and their endowments taken by the Crown in the reign of Edward VI, the support of this great addition to the church was felt to be a burden too heavy to be borne, and in 1552, a contract was made between the Bishop and the Chapter on one side and Sir John Gates then in possession of the palace on the other, that the chapel be taken down, and 'the ground made fair and plane within the space of four years and a quarter next ensuing'."

You can see the "fair and plane" ground, so either Gates worked rapidly or someone else completed the task for him, as he was executed the following year, just after Queen Mary came to the throne (see p.6).

Now walk out beyond these remains, up the steep slope, and look at the gravestones on your left, toward the cathedral building.

Dean Edward Plumptre (1881-1891)	A large slab of red granite marks the grave of Dean Edward Plumptre. Dearmer was not impressed by Plumptre's opposition to a reredos between the high altar and the Lady Chapel: "Dean Plumptre, with characteristic temerity, went so far as to appeal to the witness of the vox populi that the open view was the best."

However questionable Plumptre's artistic taste, Colchester assures us that "the personal side of cathedral life, and the Cathedral School, flourished under Dean Plumptre." Plumptre is famous primarily as a biographer of Bishop Ken, which helps to explain their link in glass - as Malden put it: "there is one painted window in memory of Edward Hayes Plumptre (Dean 1881-91). In the centre of it is the figure of Thomas Ken (Bishop 1685-91)."

Greenhalgh gives a much more sympathetic portrait of this dean. "The man who could write the great hymn 'Thy Hand, O God, has guided' would be bound to have a beneficial effect on any church". He also says that, unlike most churchmen, Plumptre had no objection to the Affirmation Bill (which allowed MPs to refuse the oath on conscientious grounds), and that he authorised the transfer of the congregation from the nave to the choir "if advisable in consequence of the cold". He also instituted "Sunday evening services in the nave in August for working men".

Now go back in to the east cloister, noting, as you go, the imprint of Stillington's chapel on the outer wall of the cloister.

On a pane of the window opposite you is an inscription in memory of a much more recent bishop, **Jim Thompson** (1991-2001), who regularly broadcast in BBC Radio 4's "Today" programme in the 1990s.
Turn left and walk towards the doorway at the end.

Six bays along, on your left, you will notice a marble tablet with a bust at the top and a coat of arms showing three red lions and three red bulls. This is all that remains of the monument to **Dr Claver Morris**, whose floorslab you saw in the cathedral. Jewers says the lions are from Morris's own arms, and the bulls from the Bragge family (his third wife).

We promised you revelations about Claver Morris, and they come from Bishop Kidder's autobiography: "he made it his business to reproach me and my family after the most virulent manner without the least injury or provocation on my part. I know no reason I should conceal the name of so profligate a wretch: His name is Claver Morice Dr of Physick an inhabitant of Wells."

Morris's first wife died in 1689. He did not re-marry until 1696, perhaps because he spent several years trying to achieve a marriage to one of Kidder's daughters. Robinson devotes ten pages to the story in her edition of Kidder's autobiography.

Hobhouse, Morris's own editor, has no text from Morris, so summarises the story as: "This lady (according to her father's account) had at first an inclination towards him, but subsequently changed her mind after a long negotiation of which the Bishop gives a detailed account, not at all creditable to Morris (if true)."

Both sides agree Morris swore: "I will never marry anyone else but you", but did Miss Kidder ever freely swear the same oath to him? Morris seems to have accused Kidder of dissuading his daughter from keeping her word, but Kidder implies that she changed her mind several times before at length "she replied that she was mistaken in [Morris]. That she could not be happy with him and shewed a great aversion" for reasons including "That she deprehended him in frequent Lies in his ordinary conversation."

The result of all this was that "When the Dr saw all his other attempts fail He wrot a letter to me in which he accuseth my daughter of light and immodest behaviour in her conversation with him. He saw he could not prevail with my daughter, and he addresses himself to another woman the following year, and begins to glutt himself with revenge."

The vow's existence led Morris to seek guidance from the Dean of St. Paul's: "The Gentleman desired to know, whether if both released other of these contracts, he could (*in foro conscientiae*) [~ in all conscience] marry any other woman; the promise mentioned being in the nature of a Vow." Kidder had a transcript of this letter, which is how we know what it said, and evidently Morris was reassured by a reply, as he re-married the following year.

Although Morris's diary does not mention this period of his life, Hobhouse has provided biographical detail and Morris does not always emerge well: "in all his three marriages Morris has an eye to the main chance. Like Tennyson's Northern Farmer, if he did not marry for money, he went where money was." His second wife, like his first, died within a few years: "She sacrificed her life in the vain hope of saving her unborn child." Four years later he married his third wife, and this marriage lasted until her death more than 20 years later.

A complex picture of Morris emerges: a doctor capable of recording that: "Mr. Hillard the Apothecary came to desire me to go to that vicious Woman Mrs. Franklin dangerously Ill of the Small-Pox; But I refus'd to have anything to do with her" but also a man who, in the week before Christmas 1724: "writ out a List of the Poor of Glastonbury who were not Reliev'd by the Parish … [to] give notice to every one of them I would on Tuesday next, be at the Rose & Crown in Glastonbury, & give amongst them Twenty pounds."

Like most others in the cloisters, this monument was originally inside the cathedral, and Robinson's extract from the Chapter records of 1730 details its precise location: "The executors of Dr. Morris are permitted to erect a monument for him at the east end of the altar, against the door there, opposite the grave where the said Dr. Morris lies interred. His executors making good and repairing all damages, and at their own expense putting up another door in the place and stead of that which will be stopped up."

Someone must have thought highly of Morris to permit such a change to the fabric of the cathedral, but you saw the new stonework when you were in the retroquire (if necessary you can turn back to page 25 to remind yourself), so you know it's true.

At the top of the seventh bay is a naval memorial to **Charles Spencer Ogilvie** of "Charlestown South Carolina" who, despite being born ten years after the American War of Independence, died "in the British Service." Ogilvie died only five years before Davis's book appeared, but Davis tells us no more than the text of the inscription and the identity of its author.

We find that John Alexander Ogilvie, the father mentioned in the inscription, was a prominent Jacobite, from Aberdeenshire. He had gone to America late in the 18th century to grow cotton (with the aid of the slaves he purchased from his brother for £800).

Why young Charles joined the Royal Navy, and why his monument is in Wells when he died in Holland (during the Walcheren campaign against Napoleon's younger brother Louis, King of Holland) we leave to the researches of better scholars. Had Midshipman Ogilvie survived he could have responded to the London Gazette's appeal in 1812: "Notice is hereby given to such of the officers and companies of His Majesty's ships hereinafter mentioned, as were actually on board between the 30th of July and 16th of August 1809, that they will be paid the several proportions arising to them, from the net proceeds of the property captured at Walcheren and the adjacent islands in the Scheldt." The Imperieuse was one of those ships. As you might expect from her name, she was captured, but not from the French in battle - from the Spanish - and while we were at peace with them. How different things were in those days!

Now continue along to the end of the east cloister (noting if appropriate that the cathedral's smart new public toilets are on the left at the far end), *then turn to your right and proceed along the south cloister.*

The first bay has a wall-mounted monument to **Bishop Law**, whose white floorslab you saw near the Lady Chapel. The fifth bay has a monument to **Bishop Beadon** (you saw his floorslab in the retroquire) and the seventh bay has one to **Bishop Creyghton / Crighton** (his altar tomb is in Corpus Christi chapel), while the entire final bay is taken up with a monument to **Bishop Hooper**, which is some compensation for the condition of his south quire aisle floorslab.

These monuments are in the cloisters rather than in the cathedral itself because, as Dearmer explains: "In 1842 … the long rows of marble tablets which had disfigured the aisles were shifted to the cloisters whence, it may be hoped, they will one day make a further journey to oblivion."

Jewers's task of documenting them was complicated by this frequent separation of the monuments from the graves, and he was grateful that "In a small work, printed in 1814, termed 'A Concise History of the Cathedral Church of St. Andrew in Wells' by John Davis, Verger of the Cathedral, a catalogue of the monuments is added – at least so it professes to be. It is useful as giving the position of the more prominent monuments before their removal to their present positions, but it is very imperfect. From the descriptions it is plain, as their present appearance indicates, that most of the accessory ornaments in the way of pillars, etc., have been destroyed in the removal to the cloisters."

Now turn right again and walk through the west cloister towards the exit.

In the second bay are monuments to Joanna Slade and her husband the **Rev. Robert Foster**. Both of them refer to his deteriorating sight, so it seems all the more poignant that the etching of the most famous view in Wells, the West Front, in the 1824 edition of Britton was inscribed: "To the REV$^{D.}$ ROB$^{T.}$ FOSTER M.A. *PREBENDARY OF WELLS CATHEDRAL &c.*"

Other Fosters in this bay, not directly related to Robert and Joanna, represent key points in British history: the inscription to Charles Edward Foster states that he "fell mortally wounded on the field of Waterloo, June 18th 1815", while that to Andrew Foster who "fell in battle on the eighth day of January 1806" records the death of a participant in the Battle of Cape Town, which established British rule in South Africa.

Look in the sixth bay (high up, on the left hand side) for a monument to Betty Sully the "old and valued servant" of the Rev. Robert Foster.

Jewers recorded three other monuments to servants, all in the cloister garth (the area enclosed by the cloisters, known here as the Palm Churchyard), but all have now become illegible.

Continue down the cloister, slightly beyond the entrance/exit arch linking the cathedral to the outside world, and go out through the doorway on your right into the Palm Churchyard.

On your left you will see that the third row of graves includes two with tall crosses. The one further from the path belongs to George Johnson.

Dean George Johnson (1854-1881)	Colchester seems not to be impressed with this dean's idea of his duties: "The major restoration of the West Front, 1870-74, was … when G H S Johnson (also a Fellow of the Royal Society) was Dean. … He did not always attend West Front committee meetings ('I knew nothing would be decided'); and he had a low opinion of Ferrey, the architect in charge.

('Mr Ferry is rather a Bungler!')"

Perhaps it was as well that Johnson kept away from this work, as Freeman is even less impressed with his previous efforts, rating him little higher than he did Dean Jenkyns: "It would hardly be believed that in an English cathedral church, in the year 1869, four stoves of incredible ugliness were set up, *with chimneys driven through the vaulted roof!*"

Greenhalgh mentions a number of significant changes to cathedral practice that occurred under Johnson - hymns were occasionally sung, and Holy Communion was celebrated every week, "but the jaundiced comment of the Church Times was that 'it would have been all but impossible to make a change that would not have been for the better.'"

Greenhalgh also shows sympathy with Johnson over the dean's stipend. Set at £1,000 in 1840, it remained unchanged until 1880 when the chapter agreed to increase it to £1,200. This had to be taken from the £5,625 annual payment (set in 1866 when the estates were surrendered to the Commissioners) intended to cover the stipend of the dean, but also those of four canons and a chapter clerk - AND all cathedral expenditure and repairs to the fabric.

Even Dean Plumptre felt that "no one could accept the deanery who had a family and no private resources". For those of us who lived through inflation in the 1970s the thought of 40 years on the same income is horrifying, but the Office for National Statistics sees things differently. Apparently prices spiked in 1840 to a level not seen since 1826, and not seen again until 1916.   That £1,000 in 1840 would be worth £91,000 today, the £1,200 in 1880 worth £130,000.

Perhaps, like Johnny Rocco, Johnson just wanted 'more', but paying the dean, four canons, a chapter clerk and the cathedral upkeep out of what is now worth £600,000 a year does sound like a challenge!

Beyond the yew tree are iron railings surrounding a few tombs.   The railings are to guard access to the steps down to "the dipping place" on the stream from St Andrew's Well.   Britton draws attention to the changes in our language over two centuries by calling this "an ancient lavatory."

Bishop Robert Eden (1854-1869)	Beside the gate you will notice the "red granite tomb, with a bronze mitre above the inscription" of "Robert John Eden, D.D., 3rd Baron Aukland", placed perilously close to the steps. Spelling is not History's strong suit, but Jewers has transcribed exactly what it says on the tomb.

Eden inherited his Irish Peerage (from his unmarried brother, a former Governor-General of India) while he was Bishop of Sodor and Man.   The DNB describes their father, the first Baron Auckland (born in West Auckland, Co. Durham), as a "penal reformer and diplomatist."

Robert's elder sister Eleanor was once thought to be engaged to William Pitt the younger, but even the DNB has found it difficult to list anything else notably about Robert beyond the fact that he "was chaplain to William IV from 1831 to 1837, and chaplain to Queen Victoria from 1837 to 1847."

That brings to an end your tour of the tombs and monuments of bishops and deans in this cathedral, but there is one more grave you really should visit.   This one belongs to a more lowly cathedral dignitary, a verger and (as you will shortly see) sacrist, but were it not for him this booklet would never have been compiled.

While you are in the Palm Churchyard, look back towards the west cloister. Just in front of the third bay from the left there is a blackened headstone in memory of **John Davis** and his family.

Jewers transcribed the inscription, then added his own appropriate note:

Sarah Davis
1824
Jemima and Sarah
twin daughters of
John and Jemima Davis
1828
John Davis
late Sacrist of this Cathedral
died January 24th 1830
aged 54 years
Also Jemima wife of the
said John Davis who died October
13th 1840 aged 55 years
(Headstone)

"He published a small handbook to the Cathedral".

Appendix

Bishops and Deans without Graves, Tombs or Monuments in the Cathedral

Complete with a Chronology,
a Bibliography, and an Index covering the whole booklet

Preface to the Appendix

Readers of this booklet in its original privately circulated form remarked that few of the deans received a mention. Seeking information on them led to the discovery of two new sources: Wharton, written in Latin, and Le Neve, who wrote in English but used abbreviations extensively. Fortunately Hardy updated Le Neve - and used proper sentences.

Although Wharton's text is inconvenient for modern readers, at least in 1691 he could make a deliberate choice to use Latin. As recently (in the cathedral's history) as 1491 the Chapter Acts record that "A certain person was brought up before the Vicar-General on a charge of heresy and holding heterodox views. He was also accused of keeping heretical books. He admitted that he could read English but said that he had not English books."

The 'Tour of the Cathedral' part of this booklet has been made directly relevant to objects visible during such a tour, so all mention of bishops who left no obvious trace on the fabric has been moved to this Appendix. Entries have been also been inserted for a number of the deans who supported or, more commonly it seems, impeded them.

As there is no need for it to follow any particular sequence, the Appendix lists bishops and, separately, deans in chronological order - that is, in order of their election or appointment to Bath and Wells.

Finally, because it seems never to have been done before, there's an attempt to show which deans, bishops and monarchs were contemporary with which, as this sometimes helps to explain the succession.

The Index covers both the Tour and the Appendix.

Other Bishops - those not mentioned on the Tour

This part of the Appendix deals with the bishops who have no memorial in Wells Cathedral. Their stories are told in chronological order.

Duduc (1033-1060) is discussed on Page 31.
Giso (1061-1088) is discussed on Page 19.

John de Villula, Bishop of Bath (1088-1122)

De Villula was described by Davis as "a man of corrupt and ambitious spirit." His qualifications for the Bishop's throne are not wholly clear, as Cassan says that "This Prelate, a native of Tours, in France, though originally a Priest, had practised as a Physician, and that probably at Bath, by which honourable profession, he appears to have considerably enriched himself." John moved the See to Bath, but he did build a palace in Wells (having demolished the canons' buildings to clear the site). Britton says that he "appropriated the entire rental of the City of Bath to the completion of his church and gave all his moveable property to the monastery there."

At first it seems that Cassan is going to join the critical voices: "The medium through which preferment is obtained is often a great mystery, and sometimes, it must be owned, it is very corrupt. ... Could the secret history of great men be traced, it would often appear that merit is rarely the first step to advancement." Having led us to expect scurrilous revelations, he adds: "I am aware that William Rufus was in the habit of selling Church preferments: however this may be, Malmsbury states John de Villula was invested with the Bishopric temp. Conq."

This highlights a problem with historical sources - William II (Rufus) succeeded his father William the Conqueror in September 1087, whereas John de Villula "appears to have succeeded to Wells in 1088", says Cassan.

Cassan's defence even extends to: "Bishop de Villula deserves a better fate than he has met from his biographers, who, instead of charging him with Simony and calling him a Quack, should rather have spoken of him in terms of respect, and enrolled him among the chief benefactors of the See."

| Godfrey
(1123-1135) |

Godfrey almost slips through the net, with Collinson awarding him only three lines and describing him as "a Dutchman, and chaplain to Maud the Empress … of him little is recorded, although he held the see twelve years". **Cassan adds that Godwin is wrong to describe Godfrey as Chancellor of England. What chiefly interests Cassan, though, is that** "He seems to have been involved in litigation, with one John, the Archdeacon, for the recovery of the lands and provostship of the Canons of Wells", **and that his efforts ended in failure. Gransden explains that Archdeacon John was the son of Hildebert, steward to Bishop John de Villula, and that the Bishop had given his steward control of the estate formerly held by the Wells canons.**

| Robert of
Lewes
(1136-1166) |

Cassan describes Robert as the "Third Bishop of Bath, and First Bishop of Bath and Wells". **He had hardly taken office when John de Villula's church in Bath burned down - along with much of the rest of Bath - so Robert rebuilt it and, says Collinson,** "ornamented it in a superior style".

Collinson then proceeds to detail what seems to have been a rare error of judgement: "Not content however with ecclesiastical concerns, he embroiled himself in the commotions betwixt King Stephen and Maud the Empress". **In Cassan's version, poor Robert** "endured much trouble, having been taken prisoner at Bath, by a party of Bristolians, and detained captive for a long time by the King in Bristol Castle. He was at length exchanged for Geoffry Talbot, one of the most active adherents of Maud".

Collinson is less sympathetic, holding that Robert brought it all upon himself when "one Geffrey Talbot, a commander of the Empress's forces, coming into Bath in the capacity of a spy, was discovered by the bishop, and detained in durance. The inhabitants of Bristol, who were strongly attached to Maud's interest, came over immediately to Bath in a large party unexpectedly, took the bishop away with them to Bristol, and there imprisoned him in the castle". **As for the hostage exchange, Collinson says that Stephen agreed to it** "with much regret, and with many severe animadversions on the conduct of the bishop, who he thought had suffered himself to be taken prisoner, that he might have a pretence of freeing Talbot, the King's inveterate enemy."

Perhaps that experience encouraged Robert to resolve the disputes within his own see.

Collinson's summary deserves to be reproduced in full: "he ordained that the bishops of this diocese should neither be called Bishops of Wells as they had been of old, nor of Bath, as they were of late; but that taking their name from both churches they should for the future be called Bishops of Bath and Wells; that each of the churches when the see was vacant should appoint an equal number of delegates, by whose votes the bishop should be chosen, and that he should be installed both at Bath and Wells. For the better regulation of the possessions of the church, he divided the estates thereof into two parts; one of which he appropriated to the chapter in common; and out of the other he allotted to every canon a portion, called a prebend. He appointed one Ivo their dean to preside over the chapter, and a sub-dean to supply his place when absent; a precentor or chanter, to regulate the choir, and a sub-chanter under him; a chancellor to instruct the younger canons; and a treasurer to take care of the ornaments of the church. He rebuilt great part of the cathedral; and dying in 1165, was buried at Bath" Cassan explains that the estates Robert divided up were those he had recovered "at length, with much difficulty" from Archdeacon John. Gransden says this was arranged with John's heir, who agreed to exchange them for the precentorship and a life interest in the manor of Coombe St Nicholas

No successor was appointed until 1174. Perhaps Henry II felt the need to be cautious in his choice to avoid another Thomas Becket, or perhaps he was misled by the Annals of Bruton Abbey which, according to Cassan, say that Robert "was present at the dedication of the Church of Keynsham, in 1171. If so, he must have risen from the tomb for the purpose."

Reginald Fitzjoceline (1174-91)

Here Cassan draws attention to Reginald's chequered past, which may have delayed his appointment: "Jocelyn, Bishop of Salisbury, our Prelate's father, had offended Becket, by whom he was excommunicated ... Reginald, his son, at first supported Becket, but afterwards came over to the King's side, and was sent ambassador to the Pope in 1171, for the purpose of clearing up the suspicion of Henry's being a party to the murder of Becket."

Like much of Cassan's work, this seems to be a re-drafting of Britton's text written five years earlier, though in Britton's version "Reginald at first supported the claims of the arrogant Thomas à Becket."

What Cassan alone offers is that "Previous to his consecration, he was put upon oath, that he was not accessary to the murder of Thomas à Becket; and others swore that he was conceived, as they believed, before his father (afterwards Bishop of Salisbury) was admitted into holy orders", which seems an unusual distinction. Sadly for Reginald, though he was elected Archbishop of Canterbury, he died before news of the Pope's assent had been received.

Savaric Fitzgeldwin (1192-1205)

Savaric became *Bishop of Bath and Glastonbury*. He was involved in some way in the ransoming of King Richard I, who had been captured by Leopold Duke of Austria. Ditchfield claims "Savary or Savaricus (1192-1205) was concerned with the release of Richard I from his prison in Germany, and was one of the hostages for the payment of his ransom", whereas Britton makes this sound less likely, suggesting that Savaric was related to Emperor Henry VI of Germany, the man who set the conditions for Richard's release.

One of those conditions was the annexing of the Abbotship of Glastonbury to the bishopric, which was done in exchange for the City of Bath. Collinson explains that John de Villula had purchased the whole city: "he was encouraged by the monks of Bath, who petitioned him to unite the abbey and the bishoprick together, and gave him five hundred marks, with which he purchased the whole city", though it was probably going cheap as Freeman says this happened in the year 1112, when Bath "had lately been burned."

Gransden tells the stirring tale of just how Savaric became bishop of Glastonbury. First the Pope moved the existing abbot to Worcester, as bishop, then he forbade the monks to elect a new abbot - but the monks ignored this bull, and in doing so had the support of the King, so "Savaric came to Glastonbury, broke down the doors of the church and had himself enthroned … the monks soon rebelled and were violently brought to order by

Savaric's party which included the subdean, precentor, Jocelin the future bishop and other canons from Wells."

Jocelyn of Wells (1206-1242) is discussed on Page 41.

Roger of Salisbury (1244-1247)	Roger was elected by the monks of Bath without the consent of the Wells Chapter. Despite an appeal to the Pope by Wells, Roger was allowed to stay, giving Cassan another chance to show the dispassionate

nature of his dislike of Catholics: "Godwin and Wharton attribute, but without authority, the compliance of the Pope to a very dishonorable and improbable motive – that of getting Roger's stall at Salisbury, or other preferment held by him, for his own nephew. Had the Pope wished to prefer his nephew, doubtless he could have found plenty of opportunities without resorting to such an under-hand mode of acting ... I am no friend to Popes, living or dead — but in all our enmities, let us, at least, be generous and true."

Freeman says the Pope decreed the Chapter of Wells should be consulted on future appointments, noting also that Roger then had "the temporalities restored to him by the King" and observing that "Henry III was the only King who habitually conspired with the Pope against his own people."

William of Bitton I (1248-1264)	This William of Bitton is said to be buried in the cathedral but no-one seems to know exactly where. Cassan discloses that "Button is accused of nepotism, or a fondness for providing for his nephews and relatives. That

many of his name possessed good preferment about this time there is no doubt, but that he provided for them all is another question, and still a further question whether their relationship was their chief, or only, merit."

Freeman says that "It was no doubt a most comfortable family party when the Bishop was surrounded by a Dean, Precentor, Treasurer, Archdeacon, and Provost, all of them his own brothers and nephews."

Walter Giffard (1265-1266), was translated to York the following year.
William of Bitton II (1267-1274) is discussed on Page 37.
Robert Burnell (1275-1292) is discussed on Page 6.

William of March (1293-1302) is discussed on Page 49.
Walter Haselshaw (1302-1308) is discussed on Page 4.
John Drokensford (1309-1329) is discussed on Page 28.
Ralph of Shrewsbury (1329-1363) is discussed on Page 18.

According to Britton "the monks of Bath elected Walter de Monyngton, abbot of Glastonbury, to this See; but as the chapter of Wells had not been consulted, his election was made void". This resulted in the post going to ...

John Barnet (1363-1366)

Barnet was translated to Bath and Wells from Worcester and had recently been appointed Lord High Treasurer of England. Fuller evidently thinks we may be puzzled by this translation, though he feels we should not be: "Say not this was a retrograde motion, and Barnet degraded in point of profit by such a removal; for though Worcester is the better bishopric in our age, in those days Bath and Wells (before the revenues thereof were reformed under king Edward the Sixth) was the richer preferment." Barnet is not buried in Wells but, from Fuller's description, it should be easy to recognise his tomb: "He died at Bishop's Hatfield, and was buried there on the south side of the high altar, under a monument, now miserably defaced by some sacrilegious executioner, who hath beheaded the statue lying thereon."

John Harewell (1367-1386) is discussed on Page 38.

Walter Skirlaw (1386-1388)

In 1386 Richard II accepted the election of Richard Medford as bishop, only to find that Pope Urban VI had translated Walter Skirlaw from Lichfield.

Ralph Erghum (1388-1400) is discussed on Page 47.

On Erghum's death, the problem of disputed authority arose once more. Britton says that "Richard Clifford, Archdeacon of Canterbury, was advanced to this See by Pope Boniface the Ninth; but Henry the Fourth, wishing to bestow the Diocese on a more favoured adherent, refused his assent, and Clifford renounced his claims; for which prudential act he was made Bishop of Worcester in the following year."

Henry Bowet (1401-1407)

This "more favoured adherent" is named Henry Bowet. "Having proved himself an active partizan of Henry Plantagenet, Duke of Hereford, afterwards King of England under the title of Henry IV, he had been, in 1398, condemned to death by Richard II but his sentence was commuted to banishment" until Henry came to power. "In 1406, he conducted Philippa of Lancaster, the King's daughter, into Denmark, to be married to the King of that country; for which services he was translated to York", which is why Bowet has no tomb in Wells.

Cassan consulted Drake for details of Bowet's career in York, and quotes: "There is nothing remarkable recorded of him in history relating to York, save that, in the year 1417, the Scots invading England, as was usually their custom when our Kings were warring in France, our Prelate, tho' old, and so infirm that he could neither walk nor ride, yet would needs go in this expedition, and was therefore carried in a chair; which action so animated the English army that they fell upon the Scots and drove them back, with great slaughter, into their own country."

Nicholas Bubwith (1407-1424) is discussed on Page 3.

John Stafford (1425-1443)

Stafford was only the second Dean of Wells (after Haselshaw) to have been promoted to Bishop. Davis describes him as "Son of Humphrey, Earl of Stafford ... he was created a Prebendary by Bishop Bubwith; afterwards he was made a Dean; and on the death of that Prelate, was consecrated Bishop of this See." Cassan remarked that "His high connections, and his great merit, seem to have occasioned the tide of preferment to flow in fast upon him", for Stafford later became Archbishop of Canterbury.

Fuller offers the ambivalent "no prelate (his peer in birth and preferment) hath either less good or less evil recorded of him.". His relations were less fortunate: "Henry de Stafford, Lord High Constable, K.G., and nephew of the Bishop, was beheaded in 1483. His son, Edward, who was also Lord High Constable and K.G., was likewise beheaded 1521."

Thomas Bekynton (1443-1465) is discussed on Page 32.

Robert Stillington (1465-1491) is discussed on Page 50.

Richard Fox (1492-1494)

Fox had been Bishop of Exeter and went on to become Bishop of Durham, then of Winchester. He founded Corpus Christi College, Oxford (and "Bishop Fox's" school in Taunton ... while he was Bishop of Winchester).

Oliver King (1495-1503)

King was another former Bishop of Exeter, but his main interest seems to have been attempting to rebuild Bath Abbey. By a happy coincidence, his nephew William Cosyn was elected shortly afterwards as successor to Dean Gunthorpe. Though Oliver King died in office, he is buried at Windsor.

Adrian or Hadrian de Castello (1504-1518)

Adrian had been Bishop of Hereford, but Cassan says he was an absentee bishop who "let out his Bishopric to farmers, and afterwards to Cardinal Wolsey, himself residing at Rome, where he built a magnificent palace." So absent was he that Hardy tells us: "He was enthroned in Wells cathedral, in the person of Polidore Vergil the Pope's subcollector in England, who also made profession of obedience for the new bishop."

Rome may have had its own dangers: "Pope Alexander having invited some of the most distinguished members of the sacred College to a sumptuous entertainment; his son, Caesar Borgia, resolved to take this opportunity to remove out of the way those of the guests, whose grandeur and riches he chiefly envied; and to this purpose, he prepared some poisoned wine: but the cupbearer providentially mistaking one flaggon for another, administered the poisoned liquor to the wicked contriver of this black design, who drank it off without suspecting the mistake."

Cassan continues: "Cardinal Adrian was present at this fatal banquet and one of the destined victims of Borgia's inhuman malice. Aubrey informs us that, having inadvertently tasted the poisoned wine, he was seized with most excruciating pains in his bowels, which brought on frequent convulsions, and afterwards a kind of lethargy; that he was obliged, for some ease and refreshment, to roll himself, quite naked, in cold water, poured on the floor of his chamber; that he escaped indeed with life, but not without casting his skin, which, through the violence of the poison, peeled off from all parts of his body."

As if that was not enough suffering: "The Cardinal was unfortunately privy to a conspiracy against Pope Leo X into which he was the more easily led, by too-fondly crediting the prediction of a female fortune-teller, who had assured him, *'that Leo would be cut off by an unnatural death, and that he would be succeeded by an elderly man, named Adrian, of obscure birth, but famous for his learning, and whose virtue and merit alone had raised him to the highest honors of the Church'*. This prophecy, which De Castello naturally applied to himself, was verified in the election of his namesake Adrian VI who succeeded Leo X."

Adrian allowed this misinterpretation to affect his judgement on more serious matters. Cassan quotes Aubrey again: "'A consistory was thereupon held, in which these two Cardinals [Soderini and de Castello], after much reluctance, especially on the part of our bishop, were induced to make a public confession of their fault, and Adrian owned he had heard Petrucci say that he would kill the Pope, but that he paid no regard to what he said on account of his youth' … he was declared excommunicated, and deprived not only of the Cardinalate and all his benefices, but even of holy orders."

Not much changed with the appointment of the next bishop, a Cardinal.

| **Thomas Wolsey** (1518-1523) | Wolsey already controlled the lands, and Britton quotes Godwin: "as though the Archbishopricke of Yorke, and the Chauncellorship, were not sufficient for maintenance of a Cardinall, he tooke also unto him the Bishopricke at Bathe, |

holding it and the Abbey of St. Albon's, with divers other ecclesiastical livings, *in commendam.*" ('*In commendam*' means he took the income, but not the job.) Wolsey's first attempt to become Pope was made while Bishop of Bath and Wells, and Britton says that it was in compensation for the failure of this attempt that Henry VIII made him Bishop of Durham, leading to his (uncharacteristic) resignation from Bath and Wells.

Cassan, quoting from "Biographica Britannia", tells us that Wolsey's first preferment was as Rector of Lymington in Somerset, where: "a piece of ill conduct, in 1502, drew upon him the displeasure of Sir Amyas Pawlet, then a justice of the peace in the neighbourhood, who carried his anger so high as to set the Rector in the public stocks of the town. Wolsey, being of a free and sociable temper, went with some of his neighbours to a fair in an adjacent town, where, it is said, his drinking to excess created some disorder, which was punished by the Knight in this ignominious durance. Bishop Godwin says, Sir Amyas treated Wolsey in this scandalous manner for little or no occasion; and Dr. Fiddes thinks he could not well justify it. Whatever judgment may be passed thereupon, we find the affront was remembered by Wolsey who, when he came to be Chancellor, sent for the Knight, and severely reprimanded him for it, and confined him within the bounds of the Temple for five or six years."

By 1529 Wolsey had reached his peak and, as Britton explains: "he soon afterwards lost the favour of the King [Henry VIII]; who, being dissatisfied with his conduct respecting the divorce from Queen Katherine, caused an indictment to be preferred against him … His fall proved to be yet more rapid than his elevation." Davis indicates the heights from which Wolsey fell: "His annual income exceeded the revenues of the Crown; he kept eight hundred servants, among whom were nine Lords, fifteen Knights and forty Esquires. Notwithstanding all his greatness, he died in disgrace November 29, 1530."

John Clerke (1523-1541)

Clerke was bishop here in Dean Thomas Cromwell's time. He had acted as an ambassador to the Papal Court, and presented the Pope with Henry's book *"Assertio Septem Sacramentorum"* ("The assertion of the seven sacraments") against Luther, which was rewarded with the style *Fidei Defensor (Defender of the Faith)* – but that was way back in 1521.

The award was stripped from Henry in 1530 for breaking with the Catholic Church and he had to wait for parliament to re-award it to him, now for protecting the faith *against* the Pope.

Wood says of Clerke: "after he had undergone several messages and embassies for and from card. Wolsey and the king, [he] was at length sent ambassador to the Duke of Cleve, to give a reason why K. Hen. 8 did divorce from him his sister Anne. Which being done, he fell extremely sick at Dunkirk, in Flanders, in his return thence, in the month of September, 1540, occasioned, as some say, by poyson given to him." He asked to be buried in Calais, but wasn't.

Yes, you have heard poison mentioned here before - John Free died of it in 1465 without quite becoming our bishop and Bishop Hadrian de Castello survived it around the time he took office.

William Knight (1541-1547) is discussed on Page 46.
William Barlow (1548-1553) is discussed on Page 2.

Gilbert Bourne (1554-1559)	Bourne was the first Roman Catholic bishop since the Reformation, and because both he personally and the church generally were in great favour during (Roman Catholic) Mary's reign, he was able to recover a substantial part of what Barlow had lost.

Fuller qualifies his approval: "we may honour the memory of Gilbert Bourn bishop of Bath and Wells in the reign of queen Mary, who persecuted no Protestants in his diocese to death, seeing it cannot be proved that one Lush was ever burnt, though by him condemned."

Bourne seems to have done many good works and had "intended to have built a college near the outer gate of the bishop's palace, but was prevented from finishing it by being deprived of his bishoprick, in consequence of his obstinately refusing to subscribe to the supremacy" of the Protestant Queen Elizabeth I, who succeeded Mary. Dearmer says he was sent to the Tower, but implies that he was subsequently kept under house arrest until he died.

Gilbert Berkeley (1560-1581) is discussed on Page 12.

Thomas Godwin (1584-1590)	Godwin was father to Francis Godwin (who wrote the first systematic Catalogue of Bishops). Fuller provides details of Godwin's early career, telling

us that he had left Oxford "for the school-master's place of Berkley in Gloucestershire, where he also studied physic, which afterwards proved beneficial unto him, when forbidden to teach school, in the reign of queen Mary."

Yea, Bonner threatened him with fire and faggot, which caused him often to obscure himself and remove his habitation."

Cassan contrasts Godwin favourably with his predecessor Berkeley, saying that "He rose in the Church not through family interest, not through political subserviency, or political temporizing, but by his own merit ; and what perhaps is worthy of remark, *he rose in spite of his merit*." He was already "enfeebled by the gout" at the time of his appointment, and "he was also attacked with a quartan ague" so that, although he died in office, he was buried where he died, in Berkshire.

John Still (1593-1608) is discussed on Page 11.

James Montague (1608-1616)

Montague devoted much effort to repairs during his incumbency, here and (especially) in Bath. He was translated to Winchester before his death, but is buried in Bath Abbey, which Fuller describes as "his fairer monument". Fuller clearly enjoys telling a tale of Montague's achievement while "master, or rather nursing-father, to Sidney College" [Sidney Sussex] in Cambridge: "When the King's Ditch in Cambridge, made to *defend* it by its *strength*, did in his time *offend* it with its *stench*, he expended a hundred marks to bring running water into it, to the great conveniency of the university."

Arthur Lake (1616-1626) is discussed on Page 34.

William Laud (1626-1628)

Some see William Laud as a martyr. He was translated to London after only two years here, then to Canterbury, suggesting he was highly thought of by Charles I, but Cassan explains that "Laud's concurrence in the prosecutions carried on in the high-commission and star-chamber courts, against schismatical Preachers and Writers, the pests of that unfortunate period, did him great prejudice with most people, such was the general disposition in favour of every man setting up a religion of his own."

Here's one example: "a decree was passed in the Star Chamber, July 11, 1637, to regulate the Press, by which it was enjoined that the master-printers should be reduced to a certain number, and that none of them should print any books till they were licensed, either by the Archbishop or the Bishop of London."

Wood does recount one unexpected duty undertaken by our bishop: "as bishop of Bath and Wells, [with four other bishops he was] commissionated to execute archiepiscopal jurisdiction during the sequestration of Dr. G. Abbot archbishop of Canterbury, for casual homicide of his keeper in shooting at a buck." Most authorities agree that Dr Abbot never recovered from this accident, and the DNB says he settled an annuity on the keeper's widow, but at least he died a natural death, and William Laud succeeded him.

Laud made many enemies among King Charles's opponents, and their petitions to parliament achieved their objective when an almost-empty House of Lords succumbed to such threats as Wood mentions: "Mr. Will. Strode (he that made all the bloody motions) went up with a message from the commons to quicken the lords in this business; and at the end of his message he let fall, 'that they should do well to agree to the ordinance, or else the multitude would come down and force them to it'." Laud was duly found guilty, and executed in January 1645. Charles I was executed four years later.

Cassan concludes: "Whatever were Laud's faults, it cannot be denied that he was condemned to death by an ordinance of Parliament, in defiance of the statute of treason, of the law of the land, and by a stretch of prerogative greater than any one of the Sovereign whom that Parliament opposed." Fuller's prediction was that "impartial posterity, on a serious review of all passages, will allow his name to be reposed amongst the heroes of our nation."

| Leonard Mawe (1628-1629) | Mawe's only claim to fame was that he accompanied Charles I (when he was still only Prince Charles) on what Britton called his "ill-advised and romantic" visit to the Infanta of Spain – "a service which", says Davis, "procured him this See." |

| Walter Curle (1629-1632) | Curle had previously been Bishop of Rochester, and was translated to Winchester only three years after coming to Bath and Wells. |

Davis shows sympathy for him, as "he was a great sufferer in the Rebellion; for, besides the loss of his Bishopric, all his private estates were sequestered."

William Piers (1632-1670)	Piers stayed a long time - particularly if it's measured from the date of his appointment to that of his death.

Piers replaced Curle, and Wood makes clear his own sympathies: "As for his actions done in his Diocese of Bath and Wells before the grand rebellion broke out, which were very offensive to the puritanical party (who often attested that he brought innovations therein and into his church, suppressed preaching, lectures, and persecuted such who refused to rail in the Lord's table, &c. in his diocese) let one of them named William Prynne a great enemy to the hierarchy speak, yet the reader may be pleased to suspend his judgment, and not to believe all which that partial, crop-ear'd and stigmatized person saith."

Cassan provides an example of these reputed offences, taken from a petition to Charles I which complained, among other things, that Piers "threatened to excommunicate the Church-wardens of the Parish of Batcombe, Somerset, for not blotting out of their church wall, upon his command, this sacred Scripture thereon written: Isaiah lviii. 13, 14. If thou turn away thy foot from the Sabbath, &c., calling it, most blasphemously, 'a Jewish place [piece?] of Scripture, not fit to be suffered in the Church;' and, upon their refusal to obliterate it, he sent his Chaplain with a plasterer, to see it wiped out, who executed this his command."

Parliament duly acted: "it is Ordained by the Lords and Commons in Parliament assembled, and by the authority of the same; That the Name, Title, Stile, and Dignity of Archbishop of Canterbury, Archbishop of York, Bishop of Winchester, Bishop of Duresme, and of all other Bishops of any Bishopricks within the Kingdom of England, and Dominion of Wales, be from and after the fifth day of September in the year of our Lord God, 1646 wholly abolished and taken away", but an ageing Piers returned upon the Restoration in 1660.

Wood tells us that "In 1660 he was restored to his bishoprick, and by the great fines and renewings that then came in, he was rewarded in some degree for his sufferings: but his said second wife, too young and cunning for him, got what she could from the children he had by his first wife, and wheedling him to Walthamstow, in Essex, got thousands of pounds and his plate from him (as the common report at Wells is) which, of right, should have gone to his said children." Clearly wicked stepmothers have existed for a long time.

Piers died in office, at the age of 94 ("The oldest Bp. in Christendom either in respect of age or Consecration" says Cassan), but he died in Walthamstow, and that is where he is buried.

Robert Creyghtone (1670-1672) is discussed on Page 22.

Peter Mews (1673-1684)	It was Peter Mews whose subsequent translation to Winchester brought Bishop Ken to Wells, so we learn much about Mews from Anderdon:

"We have at Sedgemoor the unwonted spectacle of a prelate of the Church personally engaged in the thickest of the fight. The warlike Dr. Mews, Bishop of Winchester, had fought in the army of Charles I. in 1642, and afterwards in Scotland for his son Charles II. He had also served under the Duke of York in Flanders, and now, laying aside his lawn, he once more took arms for his royal master in the battle of Sedgemoor, where 'he was active in the soldiery way.'

"Seeing that the guns were all levelled in the same direction, and that their force might be eluded by an opening of the opposite ranks, he employed his coach-horses in drawing them to another spot, and 'planted them to fire saltire-wise, that their shot might reach from front to flank.' The King presented him with a rich medal in acknowledgment of his service.

"After the battle this courageous prelate showed the true spirit of a Christian soldier in compassion for those whom he had helped to defeat. The Earl of Feversham was marching off the prisoners tied together like slaves, and making a halt at the first great sign post that stood across the road, he commanded four or five of them to be hanged upon it, and would have gone on in that arbitrary way, if the Bishop had not come up, and expostulated with him, calling out, 'My Lord, this is murder in law. These poor wretches, now the battle is over, must be tried before they are put to death.'"

Britton seems to imply that Mews's courage may have been more notable than his principles. Like Thomas Ken he had sworn allegiance to James II, but "On the abdication of his bigoted master, this prelate took the oaths to King William, and thus retained his bishopric until his decease."

In this, as you already know, Mews was unlike his successor Thomas Ken, who would not take the oaths to King William.

Thomas Ken (1685-1691) is discussed on Page 13.
Richard Kidder (1691-1703) is discussed on Page 8.
George Hooper (1704-1727) is discussed on Page 35.

John Wynne (1727-1743)	Wynne was translated from St. Asaph. Although he died as Bishop of Bath and Wells, he was at his country seat and is buried there.

Edward Willes (1743-1773)	Willes was, according to Britton, "Joint Decypherer to the King with his son Edward Willes Esq.."

Although he was bishop here for 30 years, and died in office, his other duties may explain why he is buried in Westminster Abbey.

Charles Moss (1774-1802)	Moss was here a long time, and Cassan felt he could have done more for the church in those twenty-eight years, because he died worth £140,000 and left it all

to his children - though he had repaired the widows' alms-houses at Wells. He, too, is buried in London.

Cassan quotes, from Richard Cumberland's memoirs, the suggestion that Moss's work on the alms-houses should be publicised by an inscription that "Here are five and twenty women all kept by the Lord Bishop of Bath and Wells."

Dearmer says of Wynne, Willes and Moss that "all three were typical eighteenth century prelates – rich, and mostly non-resident."

Every subsequent bishop within our scope is mentioned in the main text.

Other Deans - those not mentioned on the Tour

This part of the Appendix deals with some of the deans who have no memorial in Wells Cathedral - not all of them, as many have little worth saying about them. They too are considered in chronological order.

Some of this information comes from Wharton, but as he wrote in Latin the translations are open to challenge. He must have studied whatever records remained at Wells immediately after the Monmouth Rebellion. He says that the office of Dean was instituted by Bishop Robert (of Lewes) around the year 1139, and Ivo was the first Dean.

At first it seemed likely that Le Neve's *Fasti Ecclesiae Anglicanae*, written in English despite the title, would resolve any ambiguities, but this is no ordinary English, as expressions like "Prov. to bpc." illustrate. Hardy's revision and updating of the *Fasti*, still in English, was therefore welcome.

We have found nothing interesting to tell you about the first ten deans - Ivo, Richard of Spaxton, Alexander, Leonius, Ralph of Lechlade, Peter of Chichester, William of Merton, John Saracenus, Giles of Bridport or Edward of Cnoll.

| Thomas Bytton (1284-1292) | Wharton says that this particular Bytton left to become Bishop of Exeter but Dearmer tells us what he did while he was here: "In 1286 we hear of a chapter meeting, summoned by Dean Thomas Bytton, whereat the canons bind themselves to |

give one-tenth of their prebends for five years 'to the finishing of the works now a long time begun, and to repair what needed reparation in the old works'. The reparation here mentioned refers in all probability to the roof and piers of the transepts and eastern part of the nave, damaged by the fall of the tholus [either the vault, or the stone capping, in the 1248 earthquake]."

We have found nothing interesting to tell you about five of the next eight deans - William Burnell, Richard of Bury, Wibert of Littleton, Walter of London or Thomas Fastolf. The other three - Walter Haselshaw, Henry Husee and John Godelee - are discussed on pages 4, 49 and 20.

John of Carleton (1350-1361)

Only Davis considers this dean worthy of mention. "Bishop Ralph, finding the Deanery in a dilapidated state, obtained, from Edward III, a confirmation of a deed of gift made to John Carleton, Dean at that time, of a ruinous house adjoining the Deanery, to enable him to enlarge the same; which he rebuilt in so complete and substantial a manner, that nothing more was wanting to it for a century after." As John was Bishop Ralph's sixth dean, one of them should surely have complained to him about the deanery before this - unless, of course, they were responsible for its dilapidation.

William of Camel (one day in 1361)

We can't really class William of Camel as a dean, but he merits mention here for two reasons - both arising from Wharton's text. "Willelmus de Camel, Ecclesiae Wellensis Praecentor, ad Decanatum electus 1361 mense Septembri, consentire noluit." Regardless of our prowess as Latin scholars, we can make a good guess that "consentire noluit" means he didn't want the job (Hardy agrees: "elected Sept. 1361, but refused it"). The temptation to entrust a fuller translation of Wharton's Latin to Google suffers a blow when that translation begins "William is off the camel". William duly came good two years later when he was appointed principal executor of the will of Bishop Ralph of Shrewsbury.

We have found nothing interesting to tell you about the next three deans - Stephen Penpel, John Fordham or Thomas Thebaud of Sudbury.

Henry Beaufort (1397-1398)

Among the many political heavyweights to grace these pages, Henry Beaufort must be the only one to cast an even bigger shadow than Cardinal Wolsey. As the illegitimate son of John of Gaunt he was the grandson of King Edward III and half-brother to Henry IV. The DNB believes he was about 22 years old when a papal bull provided him to the deanery here, and shortly afterwards he became Chancellor of the University of Oxford. He gave up the deanery to become Bishop of Lincoln, by which time his parents had married and he had been declared legitimate. He became Lord Chancellor in 1403, Bishop of Winchester in 1404, and a Cardinal in 1426, presiding at the trial of Joan of Arc in 1431.

He appears twice in the wills mentioned here - he supervised Bishop Bubwith's executors in 1424, and received a generous bequest from Dean Forest in 1443, dying himself in 1447.

We have found nothing interesting to tell you about the next four deans - Nicholas Slake, Thomas Tuttebury, Richard Courtenay and Thomas Karneka, while the three who followed them (Walter Medeford, John Stafford and John Forest) are discussed on pages 38, 69 and 1.

| John de la Bere | For the remarkable tale of how John de la Bere (or de la Vere alias Dalberd) comes to be listed by some as a Dean of Wells, see the entry below on Nicholas Carent. |

| Nicholas Carent (1446-1467) | Wharton's *Anglia Sacra* devotes many lines to the tale of Carent's appointment, but uses so many unfamiliar Latin words that it is hard to draw reliable conclusions. Hardy, by contrast, just says that de la Bere was never installed and that Carent was elected soon after the death of Dean |

Forest. Fortunately Maxwell-Lyte has spread the story over four pages, from which we offer you a brief synopsis.

John de la Bere, "a collector of lucrative appointments" (e.g. the Prebend of Wedmore Secunda since 1441), had persuaded Pope Eugenius IV to issue, in 1443, a bull "specifically sanctioning the appointment of De la Bere to a deanery or other major dignity at Wells, Lincoln or Exeter, and suspending any statutes or privileges of the church of Wells that might militate against his admission there". When Dean Forest died, the King [Henry VI] reminded Bishop Bekynton of a promise to try to obtain the deanery for de la Bere. Bekynton licensed the canons to proceed to an election, and they agreed to do so … in four months' time. For this decision all present at the meeting were excommunicated by a papal mandatory, and forbidden to hold the election - but his envoy was forcibly prevented from affixing the relevant notices to the doors of the cathedral.

De la Bere obtained a royal pardon for having sought the pope's "provision", and letters patent to back it up. Several canons of Wells protested to the king, claiming the right of free election, and the lords of the Council backed their case. Carent was duly elected (de la Bere did not attend the meeting), Bekynton confirmed his appointment, and he was installed. De la Bere obtained a further bull providing him with the deanery, and went on to sue Bekynton, Carent and the Chapter. The pope ordered Carent to give up the deanery "under pain of suspension, excommunication, deprivation and interdict", but without success.

By this time de la Bere had spent 1430 marks on his pursuit of the deanery - more than the cost of Harewell's tower - so he agreed to let Queen Margaret arbitrate. She came down in favour of Carent (did we mention that he was her secretary?). By way of consolation, de la Bere was appointed Bishop of St Davids in 1447. In the bull providing him to the bishopric, he is styled dean of Wells.

In the end, we found nothing of interest to tell you about William Witham, but John Gunthorpe is discussed on page 29.

William Cosyn (1498-1525)

Although Wharton has nothing to tell us about Cosyn, despite the many years he spent as dean here, we know that he was a forward-thinking man from the existence of "Dean Cosyn's Manuscript". Watkin tell us that "the Dean had this work compiled shortly after he had come into permanent residence at Wells ... to provide a documentary history of the rights and privileges of the Deans of Wells ... Dean Cosyn could have, ready to hand, a Code of law and custom with which he could find precedent for established practice and condemnation of novel introduction."

Cosyn's election may have owed something to the fact that Bishop Oliver King was his uncle, and Watkin believes that the bishop was required to bargain in some way with Henry VII to achieve it.

In his will, written three years before his death but proved six years after it, he demonstrates great antipathy for the Archdeacon of Bath: "I have been much at cost for my lorde of Bathe and have buryed my lord of Bathe at my owne charge and could never come to any of my lordes goodes tyll the

Archdeacon was disceased, I bere all the charges and the Archedeacon was possessed of the goodes : as touching dilapidacion I ought to pay noon on my conscience for I had noon and yet I have meynteighned all charges till this day."

Thomas Wynter (1525-1529)	

Wynter must surely be the youngest ever dean of Wells, as Wood tells us that "This Tho. Winter who was nephew (or rather nat. son) to cardinal Tho. Wolsey, had several dignities confer'd upon him before he was of age, by the means of the said cardinal." Guy clarifies that at the time of his 'election', Wynter was "then a teenaged student in Paris". Wood suggests that his rise was not the only rapid thing about him, because "about the time of the cardinal's fall, he gave up all or most of his dignities; for about 1530 Dr. Rich. Wolman succeeded him in the deanery of Wells."

The next two deans - Richard Woleman and Thomas Cromwell - are discussed on pages 16 and 17 respectively.

William Fitz-??? (1540-1547)	

It's hard to believe that there could be any uncertainty over his name, but the lists all say "Fitzjames or Fitzwilliam". Anglia Sacra only runs up to 1540, but Davis identifies this dean with (and perhaps blames him for) the end of 400 years of cathedral management by Dean and Chapter: "Wm. Fitz-Williams was Dean of this Church [and] following the example of Polydore Virgil, Archdeacon of Wells, [he] surrendered the Deanery, together with the whole revenues and possessions thereto belonging, to Edward VI."

Polydore Vergil (Archdeacon 1508-1546)	

Dearmer explains that as Adrian de Castello "never visited his diocese, his affairs were managed by another famous man, Polydore Vergil, who was archdeacon, and furnished the choir of Wells with hangings, 'flourished', says Fuller, 'with the laurel tree', and bearing an inscription *Sunt Polydori munera Vergilli.*" Vergil published Anglica Historia in 1534, and Colchester quotes his account of the Wells Chapter: "there flourished a famous college of priests, men of honest behaviour and well learned; wherefore I account it no small worship that I myself, fourteen years Archdeacon of Wells, was elected one of that college."

Watkin describes him as "that many-hued eccentric M. Polydore Vergil, who live for forty years on and off in his house in the shadow of the nave, until in the end he, too, had to bow to the tempest". Vergil lived in what is now the music department of Wells Cathedral School. Colchester says it had been "rebuilt by Andrew Holes, Archdeacon of Wells 1450-70. The Archdeacons seem to have hung on to it until the famous Polydore Virgil had to surrender it to the Duke of Somerset in Edward VI's reign."

John Goodman (1548-1550 & 1554-1561)	Goodman was the first dean to be appointed after Fitzwilliam's surrender of the deanery to the crown. His presence here is inextricably linked with that of Turner (below), so here is a brief summary:

The crown awarded the new dean both the income formerly enjoyed by the archdeacon (Polydore Vergil) and the prebend of North Curry. When the prebendary of Wiveliscombe died, Goodman took that prebend for himself, so Bishop Barlow dismissed him.

Goodman sued, the Privy Council (under the guidance of Protector Somerset) backed Barlow, and Goodman was sent to the Fleet Prison, only to be released the day after the deanery was presented to Turner by Edward VI.

When Edward died a few years later both Bishop Barlow and Dean Turner lost their positions and with the arrival of Queen Mary, Goodman was restored to the deanery. Following Mary's death, both Goodman and his bishop Bourne left Wells, and although Bishop Barlow went to Chichester rather than back to Wells, Turner did return.

William Turner (1551-1554 & 1561-1568)	Colchester has particular praise for this dean: "One of the most zealous deans was William Turner, Doctor of Medicine, who had special leave of absence issued by Edward VI to allow him to preach the Gospel in any part of

the kingdom. This may incidentally have enabled him to pursue his special interest in botany, for he wrote the earliest English Herbal, based largely on his own observation and discoveries, while earlier books on the subject had largely been translations of foreign books."

Guy reports: "all that can definitely be ascribed to the years of Turner's first tenure of the deanery is the demolition in 1552 of the Cloister Lady Chapel built in 1477-87 by bishop Robert Stillington".

He does acknowledge the value of the second term: "he was able to plant a physic garden near his deanery, and cultivate herbs and plants which he used for his continuing medical practice. He was also able to complete work on his justly famous *Herbal*, finally published in 1568". Detailing a reference to a "Phisick" garden in 1673, the time of Dean Bathurst, Guy says: "it would certainly be interesting to know whether this Garden was the same as that first planted out by that other distinguished physician - dean of Wells, Dr William Turner, over a century before."

Wood seems to have mixed views on Turner: "This person, who was very conceited of his own worth, hot headed, a busy body, and much addicted to the opinions of Luther, would needs in the heighth of his study of physic turn theologist, but always refused the usual ceremonies to be observed in order to his being made priest." He says that Turner was imprisoned, then banished (for "preaching without a call") but "...returning to his native country when K. Ed. 6 reigned, had ... bestowed on him ... the deanery of Wells by the king. ... After Q. Mary came to the crown he left the nation once more ... But when qu. Eliz. succeeded, he returned and was restored to his deanery ... being then a person had in much esteem for his two faculties, and for the great benefit he did by them, especially in his writings, to the church and commonweath [sic]."

At least Wood gives us the full title of Turner's most famous publication: "*New Herball, wherein are contained the names of herbs in Greek, Lat. Eng. Dutch, French, and in the Apothecaries and Herbaries, with the properties, degrees and natural places of the same.*" He gives 1551 as the publication date, and the DNB explains that the Herbal appeared in three parts, published 1551, 1562 and 1568, so all in years when he was dean here.

We have found nothing interesting to tell you about the next seven deans - Robert Weston, Valentine Dale, John Herbert, Benjamin Heydon, Richard Meredith, Ralph Barlow or George Warburton. For Walter Ralegh and Robert Creyghtone see pages 39 and 22.

| Ralph Bathurst (1670-1704) | Colchester says that "Ralph Bathurst held the Deanery longer than anybody else at Wells. He was also President of Trinity College, Oxford, over the same period, a scientist of no mean reputation, and an early fellow of the Royal |

Society." He credits Bathurst with improvements to the Deanery building: "The upstairs front room, panelled under Ralph Bathurst ... panelling and the windows of the same room which face onto the Cathedral Green are said to have been designed by Sir Christopher Wren. But there is no evidence for this."

Guy tells us that Bathurst's wife was allocated her own seat for Divine Service. The seat was "in the grates on the south side of the Quire ... called Beckington's monument" and that the chapter decreed "that a lock be put upon the said seat set apart for her use". Wood's entries for 1673 include "Dr. Bathurst took his place of vice-chancellor, a man of good parts, and able to do good things, but he has a wife that scorns that he should be in print; a scornful woman, scorns that he was dean of Wells ; no need of marrying such a woman, who is so conceited that she thinks herself fit to govern a college or university."

Guy also says that "the aged dean, blind, deaf and infirm, died at his Oxford college and was buried in the chapel", which is why he has no grave here.

William Grahme/Graham did nothing interesting but change the spelling of his name, while Isaac Maddox and John Harris didn't even do that. At least Matthew Brailsford is discussed, albeit briefly, on page 23.

| Samuel Creswicke (1739-1766) | Guy calls Creswicke "a notorious dean of Wells. Within a relatively short period, the interior of the cathedral was transformed." He quotes from the Chapter Acts to show |

that the walls were white-limed in 1740 (presumably that's what Dean Goodenough removed in 1842,), but an Act later in the same year decreed that "two new Galleries be forthwith erected in the choir ... for the use of the canons Families". Perhaps these were the final straw that led to Dean Jenkyns' attack on the quire in the 1850s.

Creswicke later fell out with Bishop Willes over candidates for cathedral dignitaries. Guy tells us that "the bishop had a candidate unacceptable to the chapter" so the issue was appealed to the Lord Chancellor. Meanwhile the bishop "cited the dean and chapter to an episcopal visitation", but they contested his right to do so. Creswicke lodged a protest, so "he was declared contumacious [disobedient or insubordinate]" and was subsequently excommunicated. As he remained dean (with Willes as bishop) for a further 15 years, Guy's "the final outcome of the dispute is not clear" could do with elaboration, but we have yet to find a more detailed account.

Lord Francis Seymour is discussed on page 23.

George Lukin (1799-1812)	Lukin deserved a mention in the main text, as Jewers found an inscription in the cloister to "George William Lukin, D.D. Dean of this Cathedral, who died 28 Nov. 1812 aged 74", but we have been unable to locate it.

Lukin is remembered for his role in the re-exposing of the Viscountess de Lisle's monument. Davis says it had been walled up for years but "was opened by the Dean and Chapter, in 1809, when three beautiful tabernacles, highly adorned with sculpture, were presented to public view." Dearmer says it was also during Lukin's time that the medieval crozier of Wells (now on display in the Library) "was dug up in a stone coffin in the western burial ground of the cathedral." Neither of these is mentioned by Greenhalgh, who focuses instead on Lukin's relationship with the chapter, which he attempted to dissolve in 1805 when they elected a canon in his absence.

Henry Ryder (1812-1831)	Greenhalgh tells us that when Ryder was appointed Bishop of Gloucester three years after he became dean here, he was the first evangelical to receive a bishopric ("opposed by, among others, the archbishop of

Canterbury" says the DNB, adding that Ryder's brother, the Earl of Harrowby, was a prominent member of Lord Liverpool's government). His ancestry made Ryder 'The Honorable Henry', but you may care to reflect on the appropriateness of that term in view of the following:

Greenhalgh draws attention to the paradox of Ryder's conscience, which made him preach at both Mark and Wedmore, as he drew income from those parishes, but let him see nothing wrong with being bishop of Gloucester at the same time as he was dean of Wells.

Ryder later exchanged Gloucester for Lichfield and Coventry ("despite the reservations of the king", says the DNB), but+ only relinquished the deanery when he obtained a prebendal stall at Westminster.   What Greenhalgh does not tell us, but the DNB does, is that the prebendal stall had previously been held by Edmund Goodenough, Ryder's successor here as dean. Does this count as a fair swap?

That same Edmund Goodenough is discussed in the main text, on page 24.   Similarly Richard Jenkyns (on pages 29 and 42), George Johnson (page 57) and Edward Plumptre (page 52) have featured already.

The only subsequent dean to be mentioned is Armitage Robinson, who also gets into the main text (page 31) by virtue of the remedial work he performed following Richard Jenkyns's "restoration" in the quire.

Chronology of Bishops and Deans, and their Monarchs

In the table that follows, we have attempted to illustrate the length of time people stayed in office by adjusting the height of the box with their name in it. Breaks between pages interfere with this objective, but we tried.

We have used **bold type** for people discussed in the main text.
People discussed in the Appendix qualify for *italic type*.
The rest are only mentioned for completeness.

Period	Dean	Bishop	Monarch
1042-60		**Dudoc**	Edward the Confessor
1061-66		**Giso**	
1066-66			Harold
1066-87			William I
1087-88			
1088-1100			William II
1100-22		*John de Villula*	Henry I
1123-35		*Godfrey*	
1136-40			
1140-54	Ivo	*Robert of Lewes*	Stephen

Period	Dean	Bishop	Monarch
1154-64	Ivo	*Robert of Lewes*	
1164-66			
1166-74	Richard of Spaxton	See vacant	Henry II
1174-89		*Reginald Fitzjocelin*	
1190-91			
1192-99	Alexander	*Savaric Fitzgeldewin*	Richard I
1199-1205			
1206-13			John
1213-16	Leonius		
1216-19	Ralph of Lechlade		
1219-36	Peter of Chichester	**Jocelin of Wells**	
1236-41	William of Merton		
1241-42			Henry III
1242-44		See vacant	
1244-47	John Saracenus	*Roger of Salisbury*	
1248-53			
1254-56	Giles of Bridport	*William of Bytton I*	
1256-64	Edward of Cnoll		
1265-66		Walter Giffard	
1267-72		**William of Bytton II**	
1272-74			
1275-84		**Robert Burnell**	Edward I
1284-92	*Thomas Bytton*		
1292-95	William Burnell	**William of March**	
1295-1302	**Walter Haselshaw**		
1302-05	**Henry Husee**	**Walter Haselshaw**	
1305-07	**John Godelee**		
1307-08			Edward II

Period	Dean	Bishop	Monarch
1309-27	John Godelee	John Drokensford	Edward II
1327-29			
1329-33			
1333-33	Richard of Bury		
1334-35	Wibert of Littleton		
1335-49	Walter of London	Ralph of Shrewsbury	Edward III
1349-50	Thomas Fastolf		
1350-61	John of Carleton		
1361-63			
1363-66		John Barnet	
1367-77	Stephen Penpel	John Harewell	
1377-79			
1379-81	John Fordham		
1381-86	Thomas Thebaud of Sudbury		
1386-88		Walter Skirlaw	Richard II
1388-96		Ralph Erghum	
1397-98	Henry Beaufort		
1398-99			
1399-1400	Nicholas Slake		
1400-01		(Richard Clifford)	
1401-07	Thomas Tuttebury	Henry Bowet	Henry IV
1407-10			
1410-13	Richard Courtenay		
1413-13	Thomas Karneka		
1413-22	Walter Medeford	Nicholas Bubwith	Henry V
1422-23			
1423-24	John Stafford		
1425-43	John Forest	John Stafford	Henry VI
1443-46			
1446-61	Nicholas Carent	Thomas Beckynton	
1461-65			Edward IV
1465-67		Robert Stillington	

Period	Dean	Bishop	Monarch
1467-72	William Witham	**Robert Stillington**	Edward IV
1472-83	John Gunthorpe		
1483-83			Edward V
1483-85			Richard III
1485-91			Henry VII
1492-94		*Richard Fox*	
1495-98		*Oliver King*	
1498-1503	*William Cosyn*		
1504-09		*Hadrian di Castello*	
1509-18			Henry VIII
1518-23		*Thomas Wolsey*	
1523-25			
1525-29	*Thomas Wynter*	*John Clerke*	
1529-37	**Richard Woleman**		
1537-40	**Thomas Cromwell**		
1540-41	*William Fitzjames (or Fitzwilliam)*	**William Knight**	
1541-47			
1548-50	*John Goodman*	**William Barlow**	Edward VI
1551-53	*William Turner*		
10-19 July 1553			Jane
1553-54			
1554-58	*John Goodman (restored)*	*Gilbert Bourne*	Mary
1558-59			
1560-61		**Gilbert Berkeley**	Elizabeth I
1561-68	*William Turner (restored)*		
1570-73	Robert Weston		
1574-81	Valentine Dale		
1581-84		See vacant	
1584-89		*Thomas Godwin*	
1590-90			
1590-92		See vacant	
1593-1602	John Herbert	**John Still**	
1602-03			
1603-07	Benjamin Heydon		James I
1607-08			
1608-16	Richard Meredith	*James Montague*	
1616-21		**Arthur Lake**	
1621-25	Ralph Barlow		
1625-26			Charles I
1626-28		*William Laud*	
1628-29		*Leonard Mawe*	

Period	Dean	Bishop	Monarch
1629-31	Ralph Barlow	Walter Curle	
1631-32		Walter Curle	
1632-40	George Warburton	William Piers	Charles I
1640-41			
1642-44	Walter Ralegh	William Piers (in gaol?)	
1645-46	Ralegh in hiding?	Bishopric abolished?	
1646-49	Bishopric abolished by Ordinance in 1646		
1649-53	The Commonwealth		
1653-59	"Preacher" Cornelius Burges		The Protectorate
1660-70	Robert Creighton	William Piers (again)	
1670-72		Robert Creighton	Charles II
1673-84	Ralph Bathurst	Peter Mews	
1685-88		Thomas Ken	James II
1689-90			William III and Mary II
1691-94			
1694-1702		Richard Kidder	William III
1702-03			
1704-04			
1704-13	William Grahme		Anne
1713-14		George Hooper	
1714-27	Matthew Brailsford		George I
1727-33			
1733-36	Isaac Maddox	John Wynne	
1736-38	John Harris		
1739-43			George II
1743-60	Samuel Creswick		
1760-66		Edward Willes	
1766-73			
1774-99	Lord Francis Seymour	Charles Moss	George III

Period	Dean	Bishop	Monarch
1799-1802		*Charles Moss*	
1802-11	*George Lukin*		George III
1811-12		**Richard Beadon**	
1812-20			Regency
1820-24	*Hon Henry Ryder*		
1824-30			George IV
1830-31			
1831-37	**Edmund Goodenough**	**George Law**	William IV
1837-45			
1845-54	**Richard Jenkyns**	**Hon Richard Bagot**	
1854-69	**George Johnson**	**Robert Eden, Baron Auckland**	Victoria
1869-81		**Lord Arthur Hervey**	
1881-91	**Edward Plumptre**		
1891-94			
1894-1901	Thomas Jex-Blake		
1901-10		George Kennion	Edward VII
1910-11			
1911-21	**Armitage Robinson**		George V
1921-33		Wynne Willson	
1933-36			
1936-36			Edward VIII
1936-37			
1937-43	Richard Malden	Francis Underhill	George VI
1943-45		William Wand	
1946-50			
1951-52		Harold Bradfield	
1952-58	Frederic Harton		Elizabeth II
1958-60			
1960-62	Christopher Woodforde	Edward Henderson	

Period	Dean	Bishop	Monarch
1962-73	Irven Edwards	Edward Henderson	
1973-75			
1975-87	Patrick Mitchell	John Bickersteth	
1987-89		George Carey	
1990-91			Elizabeth II
1991-2001	Richard Lewis	**Jim Thompson**	
2002-03			
2004-13	John Clarke	Peter Price	
2014 to Present		Peter Hancock	

Bibliography

Author	Title	Date
Anderdon, J.L.	*The Life of Thomas Ken, by a Layman*	1851
Babington, Margaret	*The Romance of Canterbury Cathedral*	1948
Britton, John	*History and Antiquities of the Cathedral Church of Wells*	1847
Cassan, Rev. Stephen	*Lives of the Bishops of Bath and Wells from the Earliest to the Present Period*	1829
Church, Rev. C.M.	*Wells Cathedral*	1897
Church, Rev. C.M.	*Wells / Wells : in Old Time*	1909
Colchester, L. S.	*Wells Cathedral* (The New Bell's Cathedral Guides)	1987
Collinson, Rev. John	*The History and Antiquities of the County of Somerset collected from Authentick Records*	1791
Connor, A.B.	*Item 198 in Somerset & Dorset Notes & Queries*	1926
Davis, John	*A Concise History of the Cathedral Church of Saint Andrew in Wells*	1814
Dearmer, Rev. Percy	*The Cathedral Church of Wells*	1898
Ditchfield, P.H.	*The Cathedrals of Great Britain (5th Ed.)*	1932
DNB	*Oxford Dictionary of National Biography*	Online
Freeman, E. A.	*History of the Cathedral Church of Wells*	1870
Fuller, Thomas	*History of the Worthies of England* (1662, Ed. Nuttall)	1840
Gransden, A.	— *The History of Wells Cathedral c. 1090-1547* a chapter within: **Colchester**, L. S. (Editor), *Wells Cathedral, A History*	1982
Greenhalgh, Rev. D.M.	— *The Nineteenth Century and After* a chapter within: **Colchester**, L. S. (Editor), *Wells Cathedral, A History*	1982

Guy, Rev. J. R.	— *From the Reformation to 1800* a chapter within: **Colchester**, L. S. (Editor), *Wells Cathedral, A History*	1982
Hardy, T. D.	*Fasti Ecclesiae Anglicanae* (revision of J. Le Neve, 1716)	1854
Harington, Sir John	*Supplie or Addicion to the Catalogue of Bishops to the year 1608* [1653, in Nugæ Antiquæ, Ed. Park]	1804
Hobhouse, E.	*The Diary of a West Country Physician, 1684-1726*	1934
Jewers, A. J.	*Wells Cathedral, Its Monumental Inscriptions and Heraldry*	1892
Malden, R. H.	*The Story of Wells Cathedral* [3rd Ed.]	1947
Maxwell-Lyte, Sir H.C. & Dawes, M.C.B	*The register of Thomas Bekynton, Bishop of Bath and Wells, 1443-1465 Part II*	1935
Reid, R. D.	*Wells Cathedral*	1963
Robinson, A.E.	*The Life of Richard Kidder, D.D.*	1924
Turner, Rev. Edward	*Richard Kidder, Bishop of Bath and Wells, and the Kidders of Maresfield (in Sussex Archaeological Collections vol.IX)*	1857
Warner, Rev. Richard	*A Walk through some of the Western Counties of England*	1800
Watkin, A.	*A Wells Cathedral Miscellany*	1941
Weaver, F.W.	*Somerset Medieval Wills (3 vols. in alternate years)*	1901
Wharton, H.	*Anglia Sacra ... Episcopis Angliae ... ad anno MDXL*	1691
Wood, Anthony	*Athenæ Oxonienses* (1691, Ed. Bliss, 4 vols to 1820)	1813

Index

Out of deference to John Davis, who produced the first such guide, this Index uses spellings from his 1814 edition. Where Cassan, Britton or Colchester use alternative spellings, these are given in square brackets. (Disagreements over whether they were S.T.P., L.L.D. or D.D. have been ignored.) For names not mentioned by Davis, Colchester's spelling is used.